WEBB PIERCE

THE WONDERING BOY

Folio No.1

PRICE $1.00 (in U.S.A)

HILL and RANGE SONGS, INC

ICD

Elton

Song Boo

ELTON BRITT ● ROSALIE ALLEN ● DEM

ARRANGED FOR VOICE, GUITAR,

TENNESSEE YODEL P

DON'T BRING YOUR BLUE

DING DONG POLK

FIND' EM, FOOL 'EM AND F

AND 10 OTHER

INCLUDING
DUDE MARTIN'S

OLD DOC BRO

COMPLETE

WORDS
AND
MUSIC

ROSALIE
ALLEN

DENVER
DARLING

Classic Country Singers

Classic Country Singers

DOUGLAS B. GREEN

GIBBS SMITH
TO ENRICH AND INSPIRE HUMANKIND

Salt Lake City | Charleston | Santa Fe | Santa Barbara

First Edition
12 11 10 09 08   5 4 3 2 1

Text © 2008 Douglas B. Green

Published by
Gibbs Smith
P.O. Box 667
Layton, Utah 84041

Orders: 1.800.835.4993
www.gibbs-smith.com

Designed by Kurt Wahlner
Printed and bound in China

Library of Congress Cataloging-in-Publication Data

Green, Douglas B.
   Classic country singers / Douglas B. Green. — 1st ed.
      p. cm.
   ISBN-13: 978-1-4236-0183-8
   ISBN-10: 1-4236-0183-1
   1. Singers—United States—Biography. 2. Country musicians—
United States—Biography. I. Title.

ML400.G728 2008
781.642092'273—dc22
[B]

For Constance Elizabeth Green

RIGHT: Ira and Charlie Louvin.

Contents

Introduction

Of all forms of American popular music, country music especially seems to revere its roots, to hold in honor the men and women who pioneered the style long after their careers were over. Though there is less of this, perhaps, in today's modern country music atmosphere, there is still tribute paid to George Jones and Merle Haggard and others who helped shape this current generation, and it was not long ago that "Who's Gonna Fill Their Shoes?" was a popular song.

Yet this should not be surprising in the long view: When country music became a commercial entity in the 1920s, it was as much a reaction against the noisy, clanging jazz age as anything. Radio programmers and recording executives found there was a substantial market in both the cities and the countryside for music that described a simpler, humbler, slower-paced time, performed in a natural, non-concert manner.

Even this was nothing new. While mills and factories were noisily erected during the Industrial Revolution and the storm clouds of civil war gathered on the horizon, the young American nation eagerly bought the music of Stephen Foster, who romanticized about "The Old Folks at Home" and "Old Dog Trey." There has, in other words, always been a national demand for songs depicting a gentler, simpler time. There has also been a demand for songs sung with naturalness and feeling rather than musical perfection. And there has always existed the need to dance, to relax, to frolic, and to laugh.

What we have come to call country music fulfilled all those needs and demands, and beginning about

1925, it slowly created an industry of its own within the broader framework of popular music. There was plenty of country music before 1925, of course, in barn dances and roadside taverns and tent shows and riverboats and in minstrel shows and medicine shows and in vaudeville, but the twin media forces of radio and recordings coalesced then. Radio was brand new, the first stations going on the air about 1922, and while recording dated back before the turn of the century, only a miniscule amount of what we'd now call country music had been recorded before the mid-1920s. Recording machines were too expensive, the market was too small, and New York executives could not understand the appeal of this music.

That all changed after 1925, when country music became big business. For the first time, it developed stars, and these men and women are who we celebrate in this volume: the first and second generation of professional entertainers who built a huge industry brick by brick through boom days and depression, through peace and war.

Rock and roll changed it all, and the changes country music went through—the dynamic sounds and styles invented to compete in a radically changed marketplace—are the subject for another author, another book. Here we will enjoy brief looks at the pioneering men and women who were the stars of an industry they were creating. They are the country music legends of the golden era.

FACING: Rabon and Alton Delmore.

RIGHT: Homer and Jethro.

7

Roy Acuff

(1903–1992)

The sixty-year career of Roy Claxton Acuff, the long-reigning King of Country Music, nearly spanned the entire history of country music, from its church and tent show beginnings to the mighty country music machine of today. He proved to be a pivotal figure in its development in several ways, as well as one of its iconic stars.

Acuff was there as a pioneering yet transitional figure when the national image of country music shifted from string band to solo star; he was there when network radio and even Hollywood discovered country music; he was there laying the foundation for Nashville's emergence as the business center for the music and the economic forces that drive it: studios, record labels, publishing houses.

Acuff, born near Maynardville in East Tennessee, absorbed about as much music as his contemporaries during his youth; but he excelled at sports and eventually became a three-sport multi-varsity letterman in high school in Knoxville, with his sights set on a career in professional baseball. A bad bout of sunstroke followed by a mild nervous breakdown kept him off the playing fields for an extended period of time in 1929. Bored, he took up the fiddle as recreation and therapy, and quickly became very good at it. Although he never became an elite musician, he quickly found work as an entertainer with Doc Hauer's Medicine Show and then with a number of regionally popular bands out of Knoxville, including the Tennessee Crackerjacks and the Crazy

ABOVE: Roy Acuff and his Smokey Mountain Boys and Girls: Velma Williams, left, Jesse Easterday, Pete ("Bashful Brother Oswald") Kirby, Jimmy Riddle, Rachel Veach, Acuff, and Lonnie ("Pap") Wilson.

50 SONGS ROY ACUFF SONGBOOK 50

Grand Ole Opry Edition

ROY ACUFF

Tennesseans, with whom he recorded for ARC in 1936 and 1937.

He still thought of himself as the leader of a fiddle band when he auditioned for the Grand Ole Opry in 1938, but it was his singing that got him the job and made his career. His version of "The Great Speckled Bird" became an instant hit on record and on the show, and started the Opry's move from fiddle bands and comedians to singing bandleaders in the coming years: Pee Wee King, Bill Monroe, Eddy Arnold. This led to the singing star system, which gave the Opry such dominance in the 1950s and 1960s while the other barn dances slowly faded and disappeared.

Acuff and his Smokey Mountain Boys appeared in the Republic film *Grand Ole Opry* in 1940, and he made another eight films for Columbia during his War Years heyday, capitalizing on his remarkable string of recorded hits for Columbia, many of which remain the most recognizable songs in the history of country music: "The Wabash Cannonball," "Night Train to Memphis," "The Wreck on the Highway," "The Precious Jewel," and "Blue Eyes Crying in the Rain." He was named host of the NBC Network portion of the Grand Ole Opry and became a renowned star, the image of country music nationally and worldwide.

Slender and handsome, he was a fine ambassador; his tenor voice was smooth enough to appeal to the broad listening population while conveying intensity and emotion as well. It was an approach that deeply influenced the next generation of singers, Hank Williams most notably. Acuff was a little shy and reserved on radio and on film but had a fine sense of humor. His obvious love of performing was infectious and charming, and he was happy to share the spotlight with his talented band members, especially Pete ("Bashful Brother Oswald") Kirby. He also developed yo-yo tricks and suspended his fiddle perpendicularly on its bow from his chin to please the crowd.

It was also during the 1940s that he and songwriter Fred Rose pooled their resources to form Acuff-Rose Publishing, a songwriting firm that dominated the industry for many years. It controlled the founders' many songs at the start as well as huge-selling material by Hank Williams, Don Gibson, Felice and Boudleaux Bryant, Pee Wee King and Redd Stewart, the Louvin Brothers, and the Everly Brothers, among many others, in years to come.

Changing musical tastes left Acuff off the record charts after the late 1940s, but he remained an indefatigable tourer, the enduring star of the Grand Ole Opry, and an ambassador for country music in the decades that followed. He kept a very traditional Smokey Mountain Boys band in place and performed well into his eighties at his beloved Grand Ole Opry long after his touring days were over, before passing away of natural causes in 1992. He, Hank Williams, and Fred Rose were the first inductees into the Country Music Hall of Fame in 1962, a sure indication of his importance to the history of the sound and the style.

EDDY ARNOLD'S

Favorite
SONGS

NUMBER
2

PRICE
75¢
(IN U.S.A.)

HILL and RANGE SONGS, INC.
407 Commercial Center Street
Beverly Hills 1, Calif.

Eddy Arnold
(1918 –2008)

Texarkana Baby
By COTTONSEED CLARK and FRED ROSE

With one hundred albums, a six-decade recording career, twenty-eight number one singles, and more than eighty-five million records sold, Eddy Arnold ranks as the most successful country artist of all time. He was one of the pivotal figures in the creation of the Nashville Sound and the move to smooth countrypolitan music in the 1960s.

Raised on a farm in rural west Tennessee, Richard Edward Arnold received a guitar at the age of ten and had landed a radio show in nearby Jackson, Tennessee, by his teens. He spent time at stations in St. Louis and Memphis before joining the Camel Caravan during World War II as part of Pee Wee King's Golden West Cowboys, with whom he first appeared on the Grand Ole Opry. Arnold left the Golden West Cowboys in 1943 to pursue a solo career, and within a year he became one of the top-selling recording artists in America.

He had a beautiful, soaring baritone voice with great expression and range; the influence of Gene Autry is evident, but his sound was plaintive and accessible and could be breathtaking. A distinctive recording style was forged as well, featuring the simple accompaniment of fiddle and the crying steel guitar of Little Roy Wiggins.

"Each Minute Seems a Million Years" was a top-five record in 1945, but things really took off in 1946, with "That's How Much I Love You" and "Chained to a Memory" hitting the top three. Nineteen forty-seven was truly his breakout year, with "What Is Life Without Love" and "It's a Sin" going to number one, as well as "I'll Hold You in My Heart (Till I Can Hold You in My Arms)," which spent twenty-one weeks at the top of the country charts and appeared high on the pop charts as well.

Nineteen forty-eight was even more remarkable: "Anytime," "What a Fool I Was," "Texarkana Baby," "Just a Little Loving (Will Go a Long Way)," "My Daddy Is Only a Picture," and "Bouquet of Roses" all went to

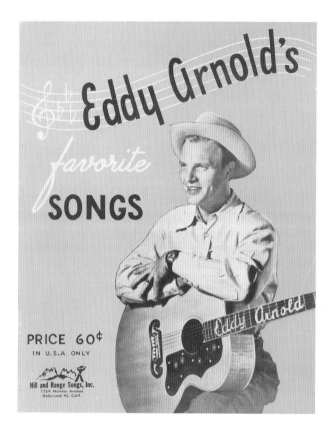

number one; in fact, an Eddy Arnold record was in the top spot forty out of the fifty-two weeks in 1948. Though that was the peak year, there were hits aplenty throughout the early 1950s, including "Don't Rob Another Man's Castle," "Take Me in Your Arms and Hold Me," "Molly Darling," "Kentucky Waltz," "Eddy's Song," and "The Cattle Call."

In addition, during those heady years he appeared on all the major network television shows of the era, toured heavily, made two films for Columbia, and even became the first country star to have his own network television show, *Eddy Arnold Time*, on NBC, later moving to ABC.

With the coming of rock and roll, which devastated the entire country music industry, Arnold's hits finally trailed off, though he charted regularly up through 1964. Still, the writing was on the wall, and he was determined to make a drastic change. He had long ago shed the homespun "Tennessee Plowboy" image with which he had started his career and forged a smoother, much more sophisticated look and sound, although he reverted briefly for a folk hit with Jimmie Driftwood's "Tennessee Stud" in the early 1960s.

Beginning in 1965 the smooth countrypolitan sound of the reinvented Eddy Arnold dominated the charts,

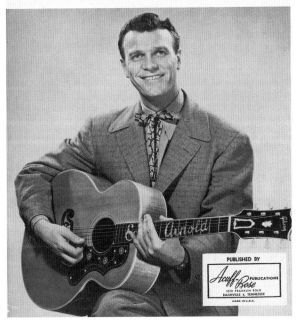

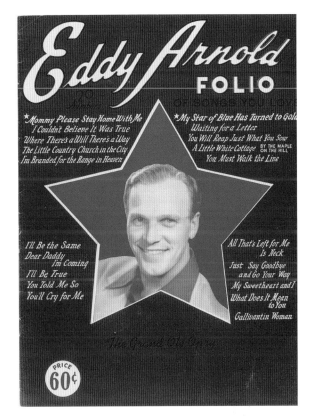

with hits like "What's He Doing in My World?" and "Make the World Go Away," which crossed over to the pop charts. Between 1965 and 1969 he began a second streak of number-one and top-ten hits, many hitting making the pop charts as well, including "Then You Can Tell Me Goodbye," "The Last Word in Lonesome," "I Want to Go with You," and several others.

Touring with orchestras and appearing in upscale showrooms and in Las Vegas, the next decades were busy ones for Arnold, though his chart successes slowed. Minor hits well into the 1980s made him one of the few artists to chart in five different decades. He finally quit

the road as he entered his eighties but continued to tend to his extensive real estate holdings and business interests. He recorded a final album for RCA, *After All These Years*, in 2005, and was inducted into the Country Music Hall of Fame in 1966.

Eddy Arnold died peacefully near his Nashville home just days shy of his ninetieth birthday.

Gene Autry

(1907–1998)

Gene Autry's iconic presence as a cowboy film star and his later emergence as a businessman and baseball team owner have tended to obscure the fact that he was at one time a rising country singer, the heir apparent to Jimmie Rodgers, one of the top record sellers of the early 1930s.

Orvon Grover Autry was born in Tioga, Texas, near the Oklahoma border, and grew up in a musical household with a singing minister for a grandfather and a musical mother. He left high school to become a telegrapher in Oklahoma but decided to venture to New York to pursue a recording career in the late 1920s. After a couple of discouraging visits where he was advised to go home and gain more experience, he finally obtained a recording contract in 1929. At that time he sang much in the style of Jimmie Rodgers, covering many of Rodgers' hits for other labels, and recorded blue yodels of his own.

As Rodgers' career was waning, Autry's was rising, and he began to develop his own sound, leading to his first million-selling record, "That Silver Haired Daddy of Mine." However, a move to WLS in Chicago in 1931 abruptly changed the course of his career, for his record producer Art Satherley and WLS executive Anne Williams, sensing a growing national interest in cowboys and the West, marketed the young Autry on the air as "Oklahoma's Yodeling Cowboy" and presented him as a pure cowboy from the West.

This approach not only began selling a great many records—such as "The Last Roundup," "Cowboy's Heaven," and "There's an Empty Cot in the Bunkhouse Tonight"—but brought him to the attention of Mascot Pictures' Nat Levine, who cast him as a singer in a Ken Maynard western, *In Old Santa Fe*, in 1934. The notion of a singing cowboy on screen was (nearly) untried at the time, and upon

making his own series of musical westerns, Gene Autry unexpectedly became a national movie star. By 1937 he was voted the number one western star at the box office, by 1940 he was voted number four among all Hollywood stars.

Many hit records followed as a result; in the 1930s they were primarily western: "Tumbling Tumbleweeds," "Mexicali Rose," "Take Me Back to My Boots and Saddle," "South of the Border," "There's A Gold Mine in the Sky," and "Back in the Saddle Again." In addition he began a long-running network radio show, *Melody Ranch*, in 1940.

By the war years, the novelty of singing cowboys and musical westerns had worn off some, and Autry returned to country love songs for popular records such as "Be Honest with Me," "At Mail Call Today," "Ages and Ages Ago," "You Are My Sunshine," and "I Hang My Head and Cry." His relaxed and friendly warm voice was as well suited for these songs as they had been for the songs of the open range and wide-open spaces. Ironically, Gene Autry's biggest hits came at the close of his recording career: the multimillion-selling seasonal records "Here Comes Santa Claus," "Rudolph the Red Nosed Reindeer," and "Frosty the Snowman," which continue to sell to this day.

Autry realized during his World War II service as a pilot that success in show business was an evanescent and fleeting thing, and though he continued to make films and records and to appear on radio and the new medium of television, he also began to build a business empire based on broadcasting (radio and television stations), oil, music publishing, television production, real estate, hotels, and eventual ownership of the California

Angels baseball team. He never formally retired, but by the 1960s he was a full-time businessman, though always smartly dressed in western-cut suits and boots.

His last major achievement was endowing the massive Autry Museum of Western Heritage in Los Angeles, a major art and historical museum that has evolved into the Autry National Center: www.autrynationalcenter.org. He was inducted into the Country Music Hall of Fame in 1969.

Blue Sky Boys

Bill Bolick
(1917–2008)

Earl Bolick
(1919–1998)

Bill and Earl Bolick were just shy teenagers when they first stepped before the RCA microphones in Charlotte, North Carolina, in June 1936, but their sound was already mature, confident, and—surprisingly for such young men (boys, really)—evocative of an earlier and gentler era, a sound well suited for the Depression. Earl's solid baritone voice and steady guitar work provided the bedrock for

Earl's sweet tenor voice and decidedly unflashy but exquisitely tasteful and appropriate mandolin playing.

Born in Hickory, North Carolina (just east of the Blue Ridge Mountains, the "Land of the Sky"; hence, their recording name), the youngsters developed a devotion for the old folk songs of their region and created a sensitive, thoroughly sincere style of harmony singing that was not only immensely appealing then as now but also extremely influential on the next generation of harmony singers such as the Everly Brothers and Jim and Jesse.

Duets were popular in the 1930s, and the Blue Sky Boys' sweet and gentle sound made them extremely popular and distinctive at the same time. Like many acts of the era, they moved from radio station to radio station and recorded actively (about ninety sides) before the war, enjoying enduring success with such sentimental songs as "The Sunny Side of Life," "Where the Soul Never Dies," "The Prisoner's Dream," and "Why Not Confess." But their enduring reputation has rested on their versions of ancient mountain ballads, sentimental songs from the previous generation, and folk songs, including "The Story of the Knoxville Girl," "Katie Dear," "Sweet Allalee," "On the Banks of the Ohio," "The Butcher's Boy," and "Mary of the Wild Moor."

And, like many acts of that era, they were called to serve in World War II and returned home afterward to

resume their career, landing in Atlanta and then in Shreveport at the *Louisiana Hayride,* and again recording for RCA. But by the time the early 1950s rolled around, their guileless, dignified sound was out of place among the honky-tonk likes of Hank Williams and Webb Pierce. Though still young men, the Bolicks retired from the road to take jobs and raise families in their native North Carolina.

The brothers were rediscovered during the folk boom of the 1960s, though by then they were middle-aged men.

They still sang as well as ever and still preserved the beautiful old songs with dignity and sincerity. They recorded again, made infrequent appearances at colleges and festivals, and enjoyed their return to the spotlight and the deep appreciation of their music displayed by the folkies and collegiates. Unwilling to pursue music on a full-time basis a second time, they returned to their quiet lives in the Carolina hills, where they have both lived to ripe old ages.

Elton Britt

(1913–1972)

Sky-high yodeler supreme Elton Britt was born James Elton Baker in Zack, Arkansas, to a musical family; intrigued by the music of Jimmie Rodgers, the youngster became a yodeling sensation while still in his teens. He was discovered by the Beverly Hill Billies band, extremely popular radio stars who brought him to Hollywood in 1930 to much hullabaloo.

There was much talk about the young man's beautiful, unerring tenor voice, and he (along with Roy Rogers) was the first to create complex, rapid yodeling patterns, using Jimmie Rodgers' blue yodels as a platform to develop astonishing vocal techniques. He set the gold standard.

He and his fiddling brother, Vern Baker, began recording as early as 1933 as the Wenatchee Mountaineers or the Britt Brothers; taking the name of Elton Britt, he also was a recording member of the Beverly Hill Billies. Britt really began to hit his stride in 1939, when he began recording for Victor's Blue Bird Label, featuring many of his most successful yodels, including "Chime Bells" and "Patent Leather Boots."

It was his 1942 Blue Bird recording of Bob Miller's patriotic "There's a Star Spangled Banner Waving Somewhere" (reputed to have sold some four million records) that made him a national sensation, however. From then until the early 1950s he charted a great number of popular songs, including "Someday," "Wave to Me My Lady," "Blue Texas Moonlight," "Got to Get Together with My Gal," "Detour," "Candy Kisses," and duets with the delightful Rosalie Allen, which included "Beyond the Sunset" and "Quicksilver." He also found the time to appear as a singer in a Charles Starrett western at Columbia (*Laramie,* 1949) and to make several telescriptions (music videos). Yodeling remained a calling card, a signature, and though he yodeled frequently on his recordings, most of his chart successes had little if any yodeling—it was that soaring, effortless tenor voice that

BLUE EYES CRYING IN THE RAIN

Words and Music by FRED ROSE

Cleared for
Public Performance
thru ASCAP

Milene Music
2510 FRANKLIN ROAD
NASHVILLE 4, TENN.

SOLE SELLING AGENTS
ACUFF-ROSE PUBLICATIONS
2510 FRANKLIN ROAD, NASHVILLE 4, TENN.

BOOK 1

Elton Britt's

COLLECTION OF FAMOUS RECORDED SONGS

Including "THERE'S A STAR SPANGLED BANNER WAVING SOMEWHERE"
Bluebird Record No. B-9000

BUY WAR
BONDS &
STAMPS

BOB MILLER, INC.
MUSIC PUBLISHER
1619 BROADWAY, NEW YORK CITY

24

had the appeal on record.

At the height of his success he undertook the first of several retirements. Having begun so young and done so much, one supposes he simply was looking for something very different in his life; he was, in turn, an unsuccessful contender for the Democratic presidential ticket, a gentleman farmer, and a uranium prospector. But the public kept clamoring for his return to music, and each time he came back, appearing on radio in Wheeling, Boston, and other markets. He continued to record for ABC-Paramount after Victor and then went back to RCA, where he had his last notable hit, "The Jimmie Rodgers Blues," in 1968, a seven-minute-long chronicle of the Singing Brakeman's life as told in a pastiche of his song titles, set to a blue yodel structure.

His return to the limelight was brief, however. Having been born a "blue baby" and having a congenitally weak heart from birth, he died of a heart attack before leaving on tour in 1972.

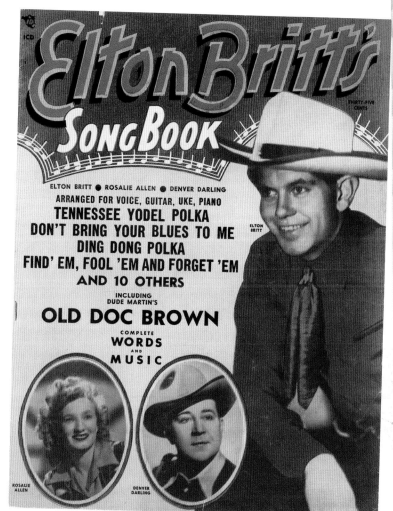

The Carter Family

Alvin Pleasant "A. P." Carter (1891–1960)

Sara Dougherty Carter (1898–1979)

Maybelle Addington Carter (1909–1978)

The first family of country music shaped and influenced the course of the genre in a broad and deep variety of ways, as singers, musicians, song collectors, and writers.

All were born deep in the folded hills just north of the divided city of Bristol, which straddles the Virginia–Tennessee state line. Fiddler, bass singer, and song collector A.P. Carter met and married singer, autoharpist, and guitarist Sara Dougherty in 1915. In 1927 this musical duet was joined by Maybelle Addington, who had married A.P.'s brother Ezra. Maybelle's revolutionary guitar styling—playing the melody on the low strings with the thumb, and then brushing the rhythm on the high strings with a finger—proved to be the catalyst that made the magic happen.

Late in July 1927 the trio took the bumpy all-day trip (though it was only twenty-five miles) to Bristol to record for Ralph Peer. Their stoic, plaintive, earnest sound was captured for the first time on "Bury Me Under the Weeping Willow," the first of many songs (some collected and some rewritten folk songs) that would become part of the core country music repertoire: "The Storms Are on the Ocean," "Keep on the Sunny Side," "Wildwood Flower," "I'm Thinking Tonight of My Blue Eyes," "Wabash Cannonball," and "John Hardy." Most featured the melodic, distinctive, and profoundly influential guitar styling of Maybelle and the haunting deep-country alto voice of Sara; A. P., more comfortable as a collector than as a performer, sang an occasional bass part to the women's tight harmony more or less when he felt like it.

The Carter Family toured occasionally and sporadically during the 1930s but recorded prolifically, eventually cutting more than three hundred sides for Victor, the American Record Company, Conqueror, and Decca. Various nonmusical work activities and the separation of A.P. and Sara in 1933 (she remarried in 1939) kept them away from commercial tours, though they landed a high-paying engagement at border station XERA in Del Rio, Texas, for a few years. There they began to

include Sara's daughter Janette and Maybelle's girls Helen, June, and Anita in the show.

A brief move to Charlotte, North Carolina, was their swan song as an act; in 1943 A.P. returned to his native Maces Spring, Virginia, to open a small country store, while Sara and her new husband moved to California. Maybelle, however, continued in show business, standing behind her children as the Carter Sisters and Mother Maybelle: Helen, the steady one; June, the funny one; and Anita, the marvelous singer. They appeared on the Old Dominion Barn Dance in Richmond until 1948, and then moved to Nashville and the Grand Ole Opry, where Maybelle became revered. June and Anita recorded prolifically with their mother, with other artists, and on their own, and toured for a number of years with Johnny Cash beginning in 1961, after June and Johnny became a couple.

Their influence as singers, musicians, stylists, songwriters, and song collectors is enormous; only a handful of other country music pioneers, if that many, can be said to have so directly affected the course of country music in sound, style, and repertoire as the quiet, dignified family from Maces Spring, Virginia. They were inducted into the Country Music Hall of Fame in 1970.

Spade Cooley

(1910–1969)

It is said that there are several treatments floating around Hollywood for films based on the sensational life of Spade Cooley, and certainly his story has far more than its share of shining triumph and dark tragedy.

Born Donnell Clyde Cooley in Oklahoma, he, like many Okies, moved to Oregon and then to California during the heart of the Depression. An exciting and technically brilliant fiddler, he found his way to Hollywood by the late 1930s, playing locally and appearing in films in small extra and uncredited roles from about 1941 on. Legendary West Coast promoter Foreman Phillips put him together with the remnants of Texas Jim Lewis' band after Lewis left for the service. His performances at the Venice Pier Ballroom became legendary, supported by such stellar band members as Smokey Rogers, steel players Joaquin Murphey and Noel Boggs, and vocalist Tex Williams.

Quickly dubbed the King of Western Swing, Cooley refined the raucous hoedown/swing-band sound created by Bob Wills to jazz and even orchestral levels of perfection. In addition, the huge orchestra—which at times even featured a harpist—was beautifully attired in snappy matching outfits, a visual treat highlighted by Cooley himself, a charismatic, athletic performer who danced and dazzled onstage.

Recording success quickly followed, with the double-sided hit "Shame on You" and "A Pair of Broken Hearts" both reaching the top ten in 1945, and "Detour" and "Crazy 'Cause I Love You" selling hugely in 1946 and 1947. Hit records were hard to come by after the departure of Tex Williams, who went on to great solo success, but Cooley continued to record for Columbia, then RCA Victor, and then Decca, and continued to lead his dance band on television for a number of years.

He had started to receive billing as a bandleader in Charles Starrett and Ken Curtis films for Columbia in the mid-1940s as well, and went on to help produce and star in three B westerns himself: *The Kid from Gower Gulch*, *Border Outlaws*, and *The Silver Bandit*, all released in 1950. They did little to advance his career but did fulfill a lifelong dream.

Hot careers inevitably cool down, and the temperamental hard-living Cooley did not adjust well to a career in eclipse. He suffered a series of small heart attacks, which slowed him down further, and, since the days of the big swing band were over, his career faded into bitter obscurity. In an alcoholic rage in April 1961, he tortured and killed his wife, Ella Mae, and was sentenced to life at Vacaville Prison.

Furloughed for a police benefit performance in 1969, Cooley performed to great acclaim, walked offstage, and suffered a final heart attack.

DETOUR

Words and Music by **PAUL WESTMORELAND**

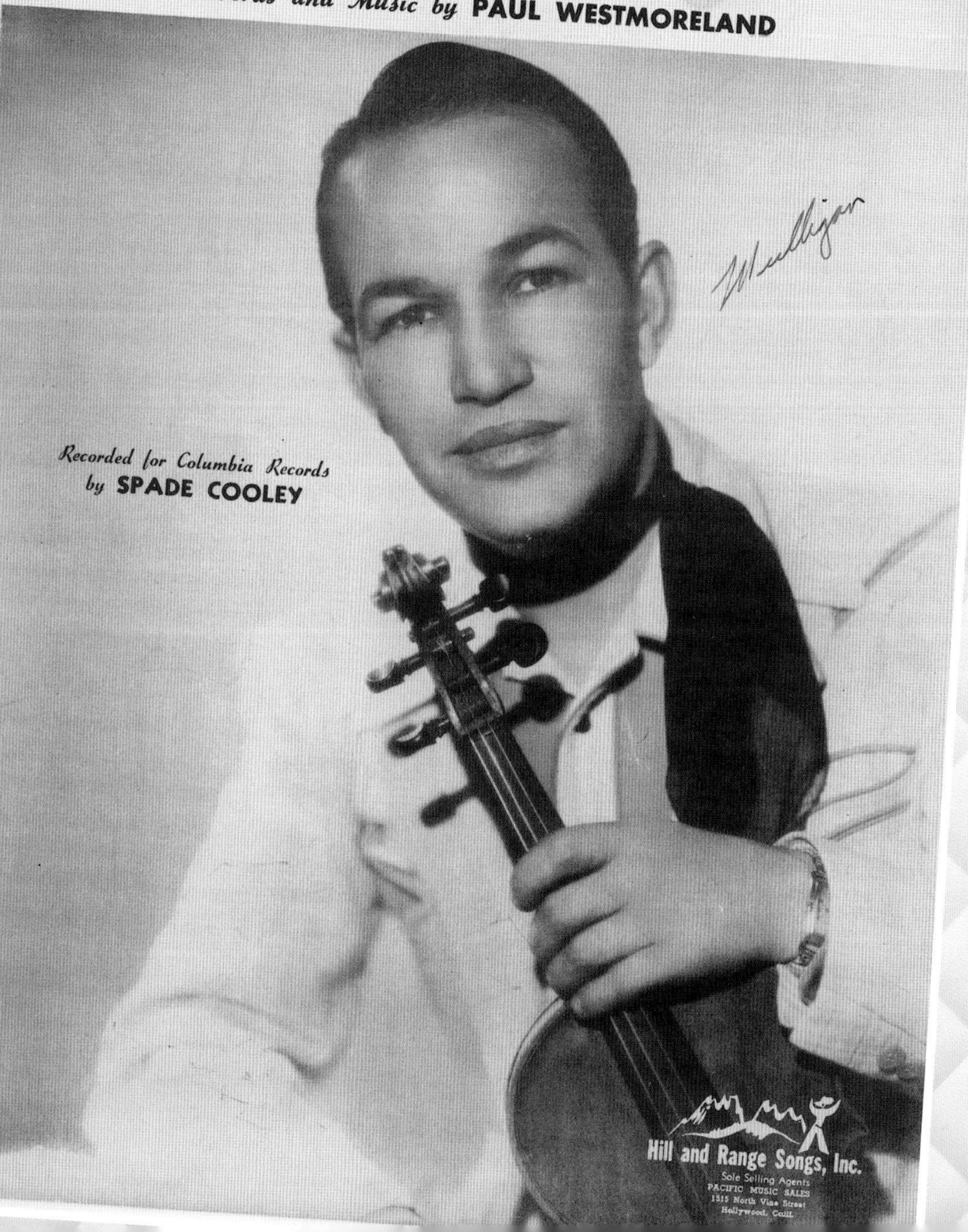

Ted Daffan

(1912–1996)

Virtually forgotten today, Ted Daffan was a pioneering steel guitarist, hit-making bandleader, and, most importantly, an influential songwriter during the war years. Born in Beauregard Parish, Louisiana, Theron Eugene Daffan fell in love with the sound of the Hawaiian guitar, and within a year of picking up the instrument, he was leading a group called the Blue Islanders on Houston radio.

Hawaiian music had had a swell of popularity in the early part of that century but was dated by the time Daffan's Blue Islanders were starting out. What was hot in Texas in the 1930s was the nascent style that was coming to be known as western swing, which mixed the sounds of hoedown fiddle and big band swing, and had no fear of adding electric instruments, including the steel guitar. Daffan began working with a pioneering western swing band called the Blue Ridge Playboys in 1934, and was recording with—and composing for—Shelly Lee Alley by 1936.

A fine musician, his greatest strength was his songwriting, and fortune smiled when Cliff Bruner recorded several of his songs in 1939, including the seminal truck driver's anthem "Truck Driver's Blues." This led immediately to a Columbia Records contract for Daffan, who put together a band called Ted Daffan's Texans, and this outfit immediately scored four of the biggest hits of the war years: "Worried Mind," "I'm a Fool to Care," "Born to Lose" (the anthem of the disaffected outsider), "No Letter Today," and his last hit, "Heading Down the Wrong Highway," which came out in 1945. He moved his band to the lucrative dance band circuit in California for a number of years before returning to Texas, and, with changing musical tastes making big dance bands a thing of the past, he disbanded in the early 1950s.

Still a young man, he founded a record label and a publishing company, and continued to write hit country songs, most notably "I've Got Five Dollars and It's Saturday Night" for Faron Young in 1956 and "Tangled Mind" for Hank Snow in 1957. Ray Charles recorded three of Daffan's classics—"Born to Lose," "No Letter Today," and "Worried Mind"—in his groundbreaking country sessions of the early 1960s, and cemented Daffan's reputation as a country songwriter for the ages.

Vernon Dalhart

(1883–1948)

Country music's first recording star was also its first crossover artist, for Vernon Dalhart came to country music from the world of light opera, and has, somewhat unfairly, been dismissed as an interloper ever since, his once shining light eclipsed by more rural sounding and appearing performers and recording artists.

It's a little unfair because Dalhart's background was every bit as "authentic" as any of his contemporaries; it's just that life took a couple of different turns for him. Born Marion Try Slaughter in the tough river town of Jefferson, Texas, on the banks of the Big Cypress Bayou where the West begins and the South peters out, Dalhart's protective mother tried to shelter him from the rowdy town by raising him on a ranch outside of town, but the headstrong and violent Slaughter clan made a peaceful life impossible. His grandfather, for whom he was named, had been in and out of trouble with the law; his father, Robert, who was at one time arrested for murder (though never brought to trial), was shot to death by his brother-in-law in 1893 in the Kahn Saloon, which still stands in Jefferson City.

His mother moved the small fatherless family into Jefferson City at that point but eventually left for Dallas when Try Slaughter was a teen. Already musical, he worked as a hardware clerk and a salesman in a piano warehouse, and claimed later to have cowboyed for relatives in west Texas as a teen. Possessed of a big expressive voice and determined to seek a career in music, he and his wife and two small children left Dallas in 1910 to head for America's musical headquarters, New York, where he again studied voice, obtaining small singing jobs in churches while working as a shipping clerk.

MY BLUE RIDGE MOUNTAIN HOME
(SONG)

Words and Music
by
CARSON J. ROBISON

Successfully
Featured
by
VERNON DALHART

Carson J. Robison.   Vernon Dalhart

TRIANGLE MUSIC PUB. CO. INC. 1658 BROADWAY NEW YORK REG. U.S. PAT OFF

Persistence and talent paid off in 1912 when he secured a small role in Puccini's *Girl of the Golden West*, where Try Slaughter first used the stage name he devised by combining the small west Texas towns of Vernon (near Wichita Falls) and Dalhart (in the panhandle), a name he continued to use throughout the remainder of his career. He then landed the starring role in Gilbert and Sullivan's *H.M.S. Pinafore* in 1914, and his career in light opera began ascending as he followed that success with the lead role in Puccini's *Madame Butterfly*.

However, Dalhart was well aware of the power of that new medium, the phonograph, and auditioned for Edison as early as 1915; and, except for his first couple of releases on Columbia in 1916, his brilliant early success came on Edison's Blue Amberol Label, for which he recorded (almost) exclusively from May 1917 to May 1919. It was for Edison that he recorded his first hit record, "Can't Yo' Heah Me Callin', Caroline?" a southern dialect sort of song popular in those days, which Dalhart always maintained was not mimicking black speech but was his native East Texas accent.

Exclusive contract or not, Dalhart began his long-standing practice of recording for virtually anyone who would have him while with Edison, and recordings for Genett, Emerson, Victor, and Columbia appeared at about this time, some under his own name and some pseudonymously. When his formal contract with Edison was up, he notched up his busy recording schedule and recorded a wide variety of songs, from light opera to sentimental to sacred to popular; by 1924 had made more than four hundred recordings.

Unafraid to tackle almost any genre of music, he decided to cover Henry Whitter's popular "The Wreck on the Southern Old 97," one of the earliest records aimed at a rural audience. He sang and played harmonica as well, and chose a reworked folk tune called "The Prisoner's Song" for the flip side, which featured an aspiring musician named Carson J. Robison on guitar. The unexpected success of both these songs—it is often stated that this was the best-selling record of the 1920s—sent his performing and recording career into overdrive.

Between 1924 and 1928 he was performing and recording almost daily—usually in the country style—and had found the perfect musical partner in Robison, who played guitar (which Dalhart did not), sang tenor, whistled, and, most importantly,

Vernon Dalhart

wrote endless numbers of songs, many in the current-events mode of "Wreck of the Old 97" (the revised and shortened title Victor had chosen), or in the country style of "My Blue Ridge Mountain Home" and "Little Green Valley." Scholars throw out mind-boggling numbers: 3,800 sides on more than 160 labels.

Dalhart's voice, though trained in opera from his teens, was a flexible instrument well suited for the early days of recording, when a strong voice was needed to overcome the sonic limits of the available technology. At times his accent seemed mannered while at other times he sang with great sincerity and feeling, and he and Robison made a fine duet team, often accompanied by Murray Kellner, and later Adelyne Hood, on violin.

In the futile attempt to avoid overexposure, many of these releases were pseudonymous, and while the recording labels obviously chose some, Dalhart also chose names of pals he'd grown up with—some black—in Marion County: Harry Blake, Jeff Calhoun, Al Craver, Bob Thomas, Will Terry, and many more. There were more than one hundred overall.

But success is fickle and decline is inevitable.

After recording almost nonstop from 1924 through 1928, sometimes three sessions a day to keep up with the demand, his career stalled out. A rancorous parting with Robison deprived him of his primary source of new songs, and the emergence of Jimmie Rodgers and the Carter Family fed the public's insatiable craving for fresh sounds. The coming of the Depression devastated the recording industry in general and was particularly hard on the country market. Though he recorded another two hundred songs after Robison's departure, by 1931 Dalhart recorded only twelve songs (though he did star briefly in a network radio show, *Barber Shop Chords*, as Barbasol Ben that year), then six in 1932, none in 1933, and six in 1934. Having been devastated by the stock market crash, he sold his mansion and made one final session in 1939 for BlueBird, RCA Victor's budget label, which didn't merit a follow-up recording.

Dalhart left New York in 1940 and moved to Bridgeport, Connecticut, where he gave voice lessons, worked as night watchman during the war years, and eventually as a hotel clerk, where he died of a heart attack in near obscurity in 1948. He was elected to the Country Music Hall of Fame in 1981.

Jimmie Davis

(1899–2000)

Politics and music are not generally complementary careers: both are time intensive and one's politics can immediately alienate half the potential fan base. And vice versa.

One musician/politician who made it work in a big way was James Houston Davis, who was born in Beech Springs, Louisiana, and became a million-selling recording artist as well as the two-time governor of his native state. Though he was raised in extremely poor surroundings—he was one of eleven children born to a sharecropper family—Davis managed to attend Louisiana College and then go on to obtain a master's degree at Louisiana State University.

Although he sang both formally and informally throughout his college years, he accepted a teaching position at Dodd College in 1927, and then began working as a clerk at the Shreveport Criminal Court the following year, which quickly drew him into Louisiana politics. At the same time he began singing over KWKH radio and landed a Victor recording contract, cutting some standard popular sides in 1928 and then a number of blue yodels from 1929 to 1933, very much in the style of Jimmie Rodgers.

A move to the then-new Decca Records in 1934 proved fortuitous indeed when his first record, a mournful tune called "Nobody's Darling But Mine," became a huge hit and a country standard. His sound moved from blue yodels to country and country swing, and during that time he served as the public safety commissioner of Shreveport from 1938 to 1942. His breakout tune, "You Are My Sunshine," became a nation-

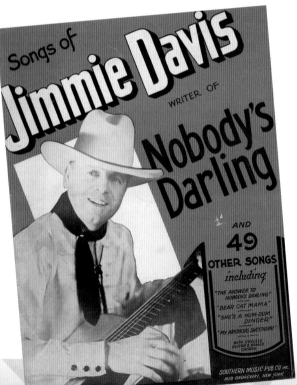

al hit in 1941, and he found time somehow to appear as musical interlude in several westerns before being elected governor of Louisiana, serving from 1944 to 1948. He even managed to star in the movie *Louisiana*, loosely based on his remarkable life story, while serving as governor.

The hit records mounted up, including "There's a New Moon Over My Shoulder," "It Makes No Difference Now," and "Sweethearts or Strangers." Once out of office, Davis began touring. The success of "Suppertime" in the early 1950s moved his singing career into the sacred field, where it remained for most of the rest of his life, although he had a surprise late hit, "Where the Old Red River Flows," in 1962.

He was not through with politics, however: he ran and won the governorship once again, and served from 1960 to 1964. Upon the death of his first wife in 1967, he married Anna Carter Gordon, a member of the well-known gospel group The Chuck Wagon Gang, and toured with her and the group for the remainder of his musical career.

Interestingly, he ran for a third term for the governorship in 1971, but this time the bid was unsuccessful, largely because of his age.

If the populace had only known, age would not have been a concern: Jimmie Davis, who continued to perform well into the 1990s, lived to the ripe old age of 101. He was elected to the Country Music Hall of Fame in 1972.

The Delmore Brothers

Alton Delmore
(1908–1964)

Rabon Delmore
(1916–1952)

Gentle, easygoing, yet subtly bluesy, the duet sound of the Delmore Brothers was unmistakable even in the era of the great duets and was highly influential in years to come. In their twenty-year career they bridged the divide between mountain heart songs and pre-rockabilly boogie, and left a lasting legacy in two very different styles of country music.

Born in rural north Alabama, the two young men harmonized from early childhood and undertook a recording and radio career as early as 1931, when Rabon was still in his mid-teens. The youngsters recorded for Columbia and auditioned and were accepted as Grand Ole Opry members in 1933, where they enjoyed great success as cast members for the next six years and had a long string of successful records for Victor's Blue Bird label. Their sound was airy and easygoing, and both brothers were gifted writers as well as singers. Adding to their unique sound was the tenor guitar for solos rather than the much more common mandolin used by other popular duets like the Monroe Brothers, the Blue Sky Boys, Mac and Bob, or Karl and Harty. Many of their early songs—like "Standing on the Mountain," "Brown's Ferry Blues," "Nashville Blues," and "When It's Time for the Whippoorwill to Sing"—are kept alive by bluegrass and traditional country bands to this day.

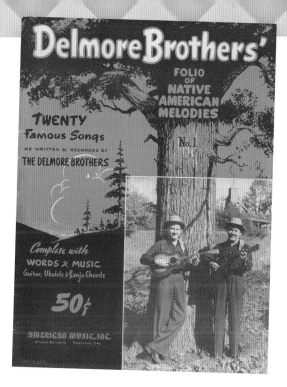

best-remembered "Freight Train Boogie" and the bluesy, dreamy "Blues, Stay Away from Me," which has been recorded by dozens of artists.

Sadly, just after the crest of this second wave of success, Rabon developed lung cancer and died the day after his thirty-sixth birthday. Shattered by this and the death of his young daughter, Alton made just a few more recordings on his own, and then retired to his native north Alabama, where he raised his remaining children, gave guitar lessons, did odd jobs, and wrote fiction and a posthumously published autobiography, *Truth Is Stranger Than Publicity,* which came out in 1977. He died of a heart condition in 1964 at only fifty-six.

Their run was relatively brief but profoundly influential, for they left a lasting mark, in their songs and in their style, on traditional country, gospel, and pre–rock and roll. They were inducted into the Country Music Hall of Fame in 2001.

The duo left the Opry in 1939 to explore other radio stations and musical territories, playing everywhere from North Carolina to Del Rio, Texas. By 1944 they were in Cincinnati, where they signed with King Records, Syd Nathan's shoestring label that launched so many influential country and rhythm and blues hits and artists. During this period they also began recording with Grandpa Jones and Merle Travis as the Brown's Ferry Four, a memorable and influential gospel quartet.

After recording in their traditional style for a couple of years, they abruptly changed course, going with a full band in 1946 and 1947 and running full tilt into the postwar hillbilly boogie craze. Teaming with harmonica player Wayne Raney, they had several postwar hits, all prefiguring rockabilly and rock and roll: the

Little Jimmy Dickens

(1920 –)

One of the great characters and most beloved entertainers in the history of country music was born James Cecil Dickens in Bolt, West Virginia, on December 19, 1920. One of thirteen children, he began appearing on radio in his native state, then bounced from radio station to radio station, appearing in Indianapolis, Cincinnati, Topeka, and Saginaw.

It was at one of these stations that Roy Acuff heard him in 1947, and recommended the small (four-foot eleven-inch) young man with the big voice to Art Satherley at Columbia Records and to the Grand Ole Opry; by 1949 Dickens was recording for Columbia and had become a member of the Opry.

Although his voice was as expressive on ballads and, later, in the rockabilly style, he began his career with a long string of hits in the novelty

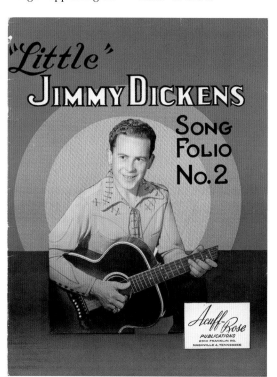

vein, beginning with "Take an Old Cold Tater (And Wait)" in 1949, "I'm Little but I'm Loud" and "Sleepin' at the Foot of the Bed" in 1950, and "Out Behind the Barn" in 1954.

In addition he began wearing delightfully garish outfits and playing the largest available Gibson guitar, which only served to emphasize his diminutive stature, and joked that he looked like "Mighty Mouse in his pajamas." A showman but also a musician with a fine sense of style, he put together his Country Boys band, which was among the finest of the 1950s, featuring twin lead guitars two decades before Southern rockers popularized the sound.

Dickens worked steadily through the punishing rock-and-roll years, and recorded several rockabilly sides himself, but made but a few ripples on the country charts until "May the Bird of Paradise Fly Up Your Nose" came out of nowhere to become a number one country hit and a number fifteen pop hit in 1965, reestablishing Little Jimmy Dickens in the national consciousness once again. Though he recorded for Decca and United Artists after leaving Columbia and had record success, that kind of overwhelming chart success never came his way again.

But Dickens remained a busy man on the road, with a sly, self-mocking, and slightly salty sense of humor and impeccable timing, which made his stage shows a delight as he mixed his humor with beautiful ballads and the novelty songs that had made him famous. After the Nashville Network came on the air in 1983, he was a frequent guest on many programs, approaching every situation with high spirits and a knowing twinkle in his eye, which endeared him to yet another generation of fans.

Age has not slowed him down a bit: in his senior years he has become a highly revered elder statesman for country music and the Grand Ole Opry, and as of this writing, as he approaches eighty-eight years old, he still appears regularly on the Opry in his gaudy spangled suits, delighting audiences week after week with his singing and humor.

Little Jimmy Dickens was elected to the Country Music Hall of Fame in 1983 and is justly revered as a national treasure.

Flatt and Scruggs

Lester Flatt
(1914–1979)

Earl Scruggs
(1924–   )

Though they may not have been precisely said to have invented bluegrass music, they were certainly there at the creation and unquestionably brought the exciting regional style to national and world audiences.

Singer and guitarist Lester Raymond Flatt was born in Overton County, Tennessee, and began a peripatetic career on radio in 1939, eventually winding up (with his wife, Gladys) in Charlie Monroe's Kentucky Partners before being hired away in 1945 by Charlie's brother Bill to form not the earliest, but by far the most influential, version of Bill's Blue Grass Boys. There he and fellow band members Chubby Wise (fiddle) and Cedric Rainwater (bass) were soon

Best Wishes From

LESTER FLATT — EARL SCRUGGS
and the
Foggy Mountain Boys
NASHVILLE **WSM** TENNESSEE
New Edition
SONGS AND PICTURE ALBUM

joined by the nineteen-year-old banjo phenomenon Earl Eugene Scruggs, born in Flint Hill, North Carolina. Monroe's soaring tenor and fiery mandolin playing defined the band's sound, but Scruggs' revolutionary three-finger banjo style and Flatt's warm vocals, strong rhythm guitar playing, and songwriting abilities (as well as Wise's bluesy, insinuating fiddle lines) made this the most influential group in the history of the style. They were a sensation—on the Grand Ole Opry, on tour, and on Columbia Records.

Lester Flatt and Earl Scruggs left the Blue Grass Boys within weeks of each other in 1948 but stayed in touch and decided to form their own band, which they named the Foggy Mountain Boys.

FLATT AND SCRUGGS

SACRED SONGS—PICTURE ALBUM

They quickly found work on radio and began making sparkling records for Mercury in 1948, moving to Columbia in 1950. While Monroe's bluegrass music was turning darker and more intense, Flatt and Scruggs' sound on their own was sunny, almost optimistic, driven by Flatt's relaxed vocals and Scruggs' powerful, exciting banjo. Martha White Flour began sponsoring a daily radio show over WSM in Nashville, and inevitably Flatt and Scruggs and the Foggy Mountain Boys were invited to join the Grand Ole Opry in 1955. In addition, they had an extremely influential syndicated television show in the late 1950s and early 1960s.

They were discovered during the folk boom of that era and brought bluegrass music to northern and western audiences that were captivated by the music's authenticity and virtuosity. This kind of national attention brought them to the notice of the producers of *The Beverly Hillbillies* television series. Their "Ballad of Jed Clampett" hit number one on the country charts in 1962, and its follow-up, "Pearl, Pearl, Pearl," hit the top ten as well the following year. In addition, they had recurring roles on the series and made dozens of television appearances on the variety and folk-oriented shows of the day. A few years later their exciting recording of "Foggy Mountain Breakdown" was used as a recurring theme in the hugely popular film *Bonnie and Clyde*, further advancing their reputation and the worldwide popularity of bluegrass music.

All was not smooth within the band, however. As folk morphed into folk-rock, Earl Scruggs and his sons wanted to continue to grow and develop with that market. Flatt was uncomfortable with this direction and was much more at ease with the traditional country and bluegrass songs and styles with which he was familiar.

A split seemed inevitable and finally occurred—unhappy but not acrimonious—in 1969.

Earl Scruggs went on to a couple of decades of success in college and folk venues with his sons as the Earl Scruggs Review, while Lester Flatt formed a traditional bluegrass band called the Nashville Grass, with which he played until ill health slowed him down in the late 1970s. Scruggs eased into semiretirement and remains the living legend of the banjo in his eighties, justly revered for taking the instrument to undreamed-of levels of virtuosity and popularity.

Lester Flatt and Earl Scruggs were elected to the Country Music Hall of Fame in 1985.

Red Foley

(1910–1968)

One of country music's enduring stars was also one of its brightest for two decades, headlining most of its major shows, turning out hit records, and appearing in films and on television as well.

Clyde Julian Foley was born in Blue Lick, Kentucky, and grew up around Berea, where he soaked up the rich musical tradition, learned guitar and harmonica, and took voice lessons to nurture his very obvious talent. Attendance at Georgetown College was interrupted by an offer from WLS in 1931, and he became part of the Cumberland Ridge Runners string band and sang duets with Lulu Belle as well as solos of his own. His warm friendly voice was perfect for both mountain songs and the cowboy songs being popularized by his roommate, Gene Autry.

Foley began a recording career in 1933 on the ARC complex of labels and left the National Barn Dance to host the Renfro Valley Barn Dance for a time before returning to Chicago in 1940, where his already successful career went into overdrive. After signing with Decca, he re-recorded one of his original songs, "Old Shep," which became his first major hit and his signature song for the remainder of his career.

He moved to Nashville in 1946 to host the Prince Albert portion of the *Grand Ole Opry* on NBC, signifying the shift on that venerable program from string bands to smooth hit vocalists. And the hits followed: "Smoke on the Water" in 1944, "Shame on You" in 1945, "New Jolie Blon" in 1947, "Tennessee Saturday Night" in 1948, and those are just the number ones; other top-ten classics of the era include "Hang Your Head In Shame" and "Tennessee Border." Without a doubt the capper was "Chattanooga Shoe Shine Boy," which went to number one in country and in pop in 1950, and helped give birth to Nashville as a recording mecca as well.

Other big records followed, most notably "(There'll Be) Peace in the Valley (for Me)," "Alabama Jubilee,"

ABOVE: Red Foley, left, with Hank Williams.

Deluxe Edition
OF FAMOUS ORIGINAL
RED FOLEY'S

Cowboy Songs · Mountain Ballads

M. M. COLE PUBLISHING CO.
CHICAGO

PRICE
75¢

his last major chart successes in duets with Decca's hot new female singer, Kitty Wells, hitting number one with "One by One" in 1954, number three with "As Long as I Live" in 1955, and "You and Me" in 1956.

Foley, who had appeared in singing roles in B westerns with Tex Ritter and others as early as 1940, went back to Hollywood for a couple of years in 1962–1963, when he landed a recurring character role in ABC's *Mr. Smith Goes To Washington* series, which starred Fess Parker. At its conclusion Foley returned to Nashville, where he lived long enough to savor his election to the Country Music Hall of Fame in 1967, a year before he died at the early age of fifty-eight while on tour in Fort Wayne, Indiana.

and "Sugarfoot Rag," as well as several popular duets with Ernest Tubb, including "Tennessee Border #2" and the chart-topping "Goodnight Irene."

Foley left the *Prince Albert Show* in 1953; in 1954 he signed to headline the new *Ozark Jubilee* in Springfield, Missouri, and continued as host when the show went to ABC network television in 1955. In addition, he scored

RED FOLEY'S
Keepsake Album

Friendship

It is my joy in life to find
    At every turning of the road,
The strong arms of a comrade kind,
    To help me onward with my load;
And since I have no gold to give,
    And love alone must make amends,
My daily prayer is while I live,—
    "God make me worthy of my
      friends."

—Unknown

Tennessee Ernie Ford

(1919–1991)

Though he was born in the hills of Tennessee, Ernest Jennings Ford blossomed in the feverish California postwar country music scene. Ford studied music and worked in radio before serving in the air force; upon his discharge, he landed an announcer's position at KXLA in Pasadena, where his powerful bass voice and homespun Tennessee Ernie character ("bless your little pea-pickin' heart") caught the ear of Cliffie Stone, who made Ford a cast member of his *Hometown Jamboree* radio and television shows.

Ford began recording for Capitol in 1948. Oddly enough the label did not exploit his warm, thundering bass voice but had him record country boogie, truly pre–rock-and-roll, featuring Merle Travis on guitar and Speedy West on steel guitar, with "The Shot Gun Boogie" being the big one in 1950, going to number one in country and number fourteen on the pop charts. His big voice was more evident on two of his other hits, "Mule Train" (his first number one) in 1949 and "The Cry of the Wild Goose" in 1950; in addition, his lovely duet with Kay Starr, "I'll Never Be Free," was a top-ten hit in pop and country in 1950.

A handsome and relaxed performer with an easygoing approachability and that big deep voice, he was a natural for television and worked as a game show host while recording during those years, having several other good records including one of several hit versions of "Ballad of Davy Crockett" in 1955. It was his stark, economical reading of Merle Travis' "Sixteen Tons" in 1955 that truly made him a national figure, going to number one in pop and country and selling a reported four million records.

From there network television seemed to be an obvious step, and the NBC variety show *The Ford Show* ran from 1956 to 1961, and the *Tennessee Ernie Ford Show* from 1961 to 1965; there were scores of guest appearances as well, including a recurring role on *I Love Lucy*.

Oddly enough, the chart records dried up fairly quickly after "Sixteen Tons," but Ford's first spiritual album, *Hymns*, became a surprise huge seller. In fact, according to the *Encyclopedia of Country Music*, in 1963 it was the best-selling album in Capitol's entire catalogue, the first religious album to be certified gold, and the first of dozens of spiritual albums he recorded through the years, assuring his enduring legacy in that field as well.

He remained active on television and with religious recordings throughout the 1970s, slowed down somewhat in the 1980s, and was elected to the Country Music Hall of Fame in 1990, the year before his death.

Lefty Frizzell

(1928–1975)

In a volume filled with artists who are by definition influential, Lefty Frizzell stands with that handful that truly shaped the sound of a generation or more. Through his influence on Merle Haggard and others, and with Haggard's subsequent influence on the generation that followed him, much of the sound of today's country music evolved directly from the serpentine note-bending and back-of-the-throat baritone of the self-destructive honky-tonker from Corsicana, Texas.

As a young man, William Orville Frizzell was so captivated by the music of Jimmie Rodgers that, by the age of twelve, he determined that he was going to be a professional singer; by his teens he had his own radio show in Paris, Texas. By 1946 he had already landed his own show in Roswell, New Mexico, had married, and in 1947 had landed in jail for statutory rape, where he wrote many of his classic early songs, including "I Love You a Thousand Ways" for his young wife.

Discovered while working in a club in Big Spring,

Texas, in 1950, his songs were sent to Don Law in Nashville, who was interested in "If You've Got the Money I've Got the Time" for Little Jimmy Dickens.

But Law heard something very special in the demo by the young songwriter and signed Frizzell to Columbia in June 1950. Those two songs were put on each side of his first record, and each went to number one on the charts late in 1950.

A wave of hits followed in the next couple of years, including "I Want to Be with You Always," "Look What Thoughts Will Do," "Mom and Dad's Waltz," "Traveling Blues," "How Long Will It Take," and the definitive example of his revolutionary vocal style, "Always Late (with Your Kisses)." Frizzell toured with Hank Williams and joined the Opry in 1951, his breakout year, but his excessive self-destructive lifestyle continued to get in his way. There were more scrapes with the law, legal problems over several conflicting management contracts, and problems with alcohol; by 1954 his meteoric rise to the top was over, and, though still a very young man, his glory days had slipped past him.

Frizzell moved to Southern California in 1955,

finding the atmosphere freer there than in the South, and remained quite busy in clubs and concerts, though he had no hit records of any kind for several years. He enjoyed something of a comeback during the folk boom with his classic, stark hit version of "The Long Black Veil" in 1959, and returned to the Nashville area in 1962. His last number one record was another story song, Bill Anderson's humorously ironic "Saginaw, Michigan" in 1964. Though he continued to record well into the 1970s (including the now classic "Gone, Gone, Gone" in 1965) he was no longer a presence on the charts after this point, which was depressing indeed for a man who was not only well aware of his talent and influence but also in his late thirties and early forties.

He began to concentrate once again on his songwriting in those years, often teaming up with Whitey Shafer, with whom he wrote the enduring songs "That's the Way Love Goes" and "I Never Go Around Mirrors," but a lifetime of heavy drinking and high blood pressure led to a sudden fatal stroke that ended his troubled life at the age of forty-seven.

He was inducted into the Country Music Hall of Fame in 1982.

Homer and Jethro

Henry Haynes
(1920–1971)

Kenneth Burns
(1920–1989)

While much of the world knew them as wisecracking hayseeds who tortured the lyrics to popular country songs, every musician who ever heard them recognized them as among the finest swing musicians country music ever produced.

The two had met as teens while auditioning for the Midday Merry Go Round in Knoxville in the early 1930s, and when a forgetful announcer introduced them as Homer and Jethro, the teenagers immediately adopted the mistaken names. First playing as part of the String Dusters string band, the two went on their own as a duet when the String Dusters disbanded, a move that only lasted until World War II separated them for years. They reunited at WLW in Cincinnati upon release from the service and began recording there for King Records in 1946, where they played as staff musicians for many of King's artists as well as recorded on their own.

Although they began in devoted imitation of brother groups like the Blue Sky Boys, their amusing onstage presence and their knack for making cornball parodies of popular and country songs quickly categorized them as a comedy act, despite the swingy jazz phrasing of

Jethro's mandolin and Homer's gold-standard swing rhythm guitar work. They had the magic ability to be relentlessly corny while being completely hip at the same time. Regional hits of this type on King brought them to the attention of RCA Victor in 1949, where they scored a top-ten hit of "Baby, It's Cold Outside" with June Carter. Sporadic hits followed in the 1950s, including "Tennessee Border #2" in 1949; their biggest, "(How Much Is) that Hound Dog in the Window," in 1953; "Hernando's Hideaway" in 1954; and "The Battle of Kookamonga" in 1959. The self-styled

McNeill's Breakfast Club. Though they did not have hit records in the 1960s, their national exposure was wide indeed, not only from appearances on most of the network variety specials, but also from two ubiquitous ad campaigns for Kellogg's Corn Flakes ("Corniest Flakes Anybody Makes"). After the release of their live album *Homer and Jethro Live at the Country Club* in 1960, they became almost exclusively an album act, and their non-comedy instrumental albums, *It Ain't Necessarily Square,* *Playing It Straight,* and *Tenderly and Other Great Love Ballads* are true classics of country swing. They were sailing high when Homer, the undisputed master of the rhythm guitar, died unexpectedly just two weeks after his fifty-first birthday, in 1971.

A devastated Jethro remained inactive for a time but was eventually coaxed into a second career as a jazz soloist and elder statesman of the mandolin by young blue grass musicians who were inspired and enthralled by his technique and phrasing. He toured folk clubs and festivals until his own fatal illness finally halted his long career in the late 1980s. They were inducted into the Country Music Hall of Fame in 2001.

"song butchers" also had their satiric way with parodies such as "Don't Let the Stars Get in Your Eyeballs," "Let Me Go, Blubber," "The Ballad of Davy Crewcut," and on and on.

The duo had joined WLS in Chicago in 1950 and made the Windy City their base of operations as they appeared on the *National Barn Dance* and on *Don*

Hoosier Hot Shots

Ken Trietsch (1903–1987) **Paul "Hezzie" Trietsch** (1905–1979) **Charles "Gabe" Ward** (1904–1992) **Frank Kettering** (1909–1973) **Gil Taylor** (unknown)

(later members included Nate Harrison and Keith Milheim)

Hugely popular in their day, and largely forgotten today, this madcap quartet with the famous tagline "Are you ready, Hezzie?" was a rural sensation in the 1930s and 1940s. Armed with Hezzie's tin whistle and washboard, they were known for an endless string of novelty songs like "I Like Bananas Because They Have No Bones," and "From the Indes to the Andes in His Undies," delivered in sassy, devil-may-care style.

Ken (on tenor guitar) and Paul Trietsch, both from northern Indiana, teamed up with fellow Hoosier Gabe Ward, a fine clarinetist, and played novelty songs on the vaudeville circuit before adding bassist Frank Kettering in 1933 and joining the *National Barn Dance*. They began recording for the American Record Corporation's galaxy of labels (Banner, Oriole, Romeo, Conqueror, etc.) in 1934, and eventually had more than one hundred sides released in their long career.

They headed west to begin appearing in films in the late 1930s, their first credited role being in Gene Autry's *In Old Monterey* in 1939, and they also had a large role in Paramount's *The National Barn Dance* in 1944. They starred in *Hoosier Holiday* for Republic in 1942 (featuring a young Dale Evans in pre—Roy Rogers days), and provided musical support for Ken Curtis in his musical westerns for Columbia from 1945 to 1947, when smooth vocalist and bassist Gil Taylor replaced Kettering in the lineup. They even launched their own series for Columbia, with a handful of films like *Swing the Western Way* (1947), *Singin' Spurs* (1948), *Rose of Santa Rosa* (1948), and *The Arkansas Swing* (Republic, 1949), and resettled in Southern California during these heady years.

Their recording career was similarly hot during this time; they scored three top-ten hits after switching to the Decca label: "She Broke My Heart in Three Places" in 1944; "Someday (You'll Want Me to Want You)," a duet by Gil Taylor and Sally Foster in 1946; and "Sioux City Sue" the same year. They also hosted their own Mutual Radio Network program *The Hoosier Hot Shot Show* in the early 1950s. This was their peak, and while they continued to record well into the 1960s, their career curve had reached its apex and settled back; they remained busy on tour and in Nevada nightclubs up until Hezzie's untimely death in 1980. Only Gabe Ward remained active after that, crafting a career as an after-dinner speaker and playing clarinet with a quartet.

Their sound was raucous and rowdy, a huge inspiration to Spike Jones when he created his City Slickers, and unique in the annals of country music history.

ABOVE: (Clockwise from top) Paul Trietsch, Ken Trietsch, Gil Taylor, and Gabe Ward.

Grandpa Jones

(1913–1998)

A grandpa from the age of twenty-two—on stage, of course—Grandpa Jones was an untiring devotee of old-time music from his earliest years, when he first appeared on radio as the "Young Singer of Old Songs." This first nickname didn't stick, but it did clearly define his lifelong musical orientation.

Louis Marshall Jones was from that fertile northwest area of Kentucky that produced such other legendary figures as Bill and Charlie Monroe, Merle Travis, Ike Everly and his sons Don and Phil, and many others. The family moved to Akron, Ohio, when Marshall (as he was then called) was a teen, and through a fellow musician he met Bradley Kincaid, who hired the youngster in 1935, brought him to WBZ in Boston, outfitted him in lace-up boots, battered hat, and fake mustache, and nicknamed him Grandpa.

Jones launched his solo career in 1937, learned to play claw hammer banjo from Cousin Emmy along the way, and wound up at WLW in Cincinnati, where he became a fixture of the then-thriving music scene. A lover of old-time southern gospel music as well as mountain songs, he began recording for the brand-new King label with Merle Travis and the Delmore Brothers as the Brown's Ferry Four. Throughout the remainder of the 1940s he recorded prolifically for King, scoring his most memorable hits: "It's Raining Here this Morning," "Eight More Miles to Louisville," "Rattler," and "Mountain Dew."

Grandpa Jones joined the Grand Ole Opry after his return from service in 1946, left, and then returned after stays in Richmond and Washington, D.C. He moved to RCA Records in 1952

Harmonies of the Hill Country

by Grandpa Jones

and then to Decca in the late 1950s. While he had successful records, it was on radio and in personal appearances that he forged a lasting career. His only real top-ten record came surprisingly late—1962—in a rerecording of Jimmie Rodgers' "Blue Yodel," for the upstart Monument Label.

Throughout his career Jones had been primarily a singer and musician, but his wry, razor-edged sense of humor and dry, sardonic delivery made him one of the funniest men in the music's history, on- or offstage. Indeed, Grandpa Jones quips are still circulated to this day among the older generation of musicians.

It was far more as a humorist than as a banjo picker or singer (though he did plenty of both) that he was hired for the cast of *Hee Haw* in 1969, and this convivial atmosphere introduced him to a whole new generation. At the same time, he began recording a series of albums with his talented wife, Ramona, and their two equally talented children for the independent CMH label.

As he aged into his costume (his big fake silver mustache was eventually replaced with a smaller silver real one) he continued to champion old-time music and traditional songs and styles, and became an elder statesman for country music's rich history. He was elected to the Country Music Hall of Fame in 1978, published an autobiography in 1984, and suffered a stroke shortly after walking offstage at his beloved Grand Ole Opry in 1998.

ABOVE: Grandpa Jones, center.

Bradley Kincaid

(1895–1989)

One might well suspect that the era of the folk song collector and scholar/performer began with the folk song revival of the late 1950s and early 1960s, but Bradley Kincaid was there at the beginning.

Born at Point Leavell, Kentucky, he was educated at the Berea Academy, where he was instilled with a love of the ancient folk music of the Appalachians and a desire to preserve it. What he had as well was a lovely tenor voice well suited to presenting those ballads, and an old guitar his father traded a hunting dog for; hence, his famous "Hound Dog Guitar."

Kincaid traveled to Chicago to attend the YMCA College from 1924 to 1928, but while there he discovered a radio market hungry for aged ballads like "Barbara Allen," which he had been collecting for years. He quickly became one of the earliest stars of radio after landing a show on WLS and was the first country radio star to publish a songbook, which sold well over one hundred thousand copies. It became the first of many and prompted several collecting trips into the Kentucky hills to uncover more ancient treasures. Only A. P. Carter collected as diligently, and only Tex Ritter (in the cowboy field) rivaled Kincaid's extensive knowledge and folkloric approach to the classic material.

Kincaid began recording during his 1926–1929 stay at WLS, initially recording for Gennett Records and eventually cutting more than one hundred sides for Brunswick, Bluebird, Decca, and Capitol in his long career. He began the pattern of moving from station to station that marked his performing career when he moved to WLW in Cincinnati in 1930. He lasted about a year there before moving to WGY in Schenectady, and then remained about a year, doing radio and personal appearances, at each of the following stations: WEAF in New York City

Best wishes to
Joe Frank
Bradley Kincaid
WLS
1931

Theatrical
CHICAGO

My Favorite Old Time Songs and Mountain Ballads

Bradley Kincaid

(where he was featured on the NBC network as well), WBZ in Boston, WTIC in Hartford, back to WGY, and then to WHAM in Rochester. It was during this hectic 1930s era that he worked with—and nicknamed—Grandpa Jones. Much of the interest in folk song and country music in the Northeast can be traced to Kincaid's long visit to that region.

It was back to Cincinnati from 1941 to 1944 and then on to the Grand Ole Opry in Nashville from 1945 to 1950; there he was immortalized in "The Grand Ole Opry Song": "None can sing the old songs like Bradley Kincaid." He scarcely needed immortalizing, however, for by this time he had taught a generation the folk songs that did indeed pave the way for the folk revival a few years later.

But in 1950 he realized his days of popularizing while preserving the ancient ballads was over. The newer, slicker, big band and honky-tonk sound was dominating the Opry and the airwaves, while his gentle folk songs were no longer a novelty. He had never tried or cared to keep up with contemporary sounds, styles, and songs; he remained true to the ballads he had sung as a youth and collected as a young man, and very few newly

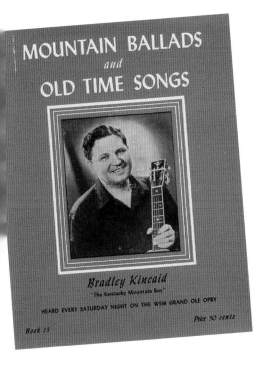

composed songs—and even those were of very traditional character—ever made it into his repertoire. His stock in trade remained "Sourwood Mountain," "A Paper of Pins," "Pretty Little Pink," and, of course, the classic "Barbara Allen."

Bradley Kincaid retired gracefully, buying into a radio station and later a music store in Springfield, Ohio, where he lived to a ripe old age.

Pee Wee King

(1914–2000)

Influential in many ways as a bandleader, Pee Wee King will doubtless always be best remembered for his songwriting, usually in collaboration with his longtime partner Redd Stewart.

Born in Wisconsin, Frank Julius Anthony Kuczynski grew up in a fertile musical environment and was playing with his father's polka band by the time he reached his teens. He formed his own band in high school and joined the Badger State Barn Dance, where he changed his stage name to Frankie King. It was there he was discovered by up-and-coming promoter and businessman J. L. Frank, who moved him to Louisville in 1934 to back up Gene Autry, who had moved there briefly after leaving WLS in Chicago before heading to Hollywood to make westerns; it was Autry who nicknamed the skinny five-and-a-half-foot accordionist "Pee Wee."

With musical westerns becoming increasingly popular, King changed the name of his band to the Golden West Cowboys and dressed them in sharp western outfits. They joined the Grand Ole Opry in 1937, where they brought a modern dance-band sound to the stage formerly occupied almost exclusively by string bands and sentimental singers, and pioneered the use of unfamiliar instruments and sounds on that program, including trumpets, drums, and electric guitars. In addition, a number of talented singers passed through the band during those years, including Eddy Arnold and Cowboy Copas.

Although extremely popular on the Opry, it was only after he left in 1947 that his biggest

FACING: Pee Wee King and his Golden West Cowboys: King, far left, and at his right are Smiley Burnette and Carolina Cotton, while Redd Stewart fiddles at the far right.

Pee Wee King

successes came. King signed with RCA Victor in 1947, and a succession of fine hit records followed, including the all-time classic "Tennessee Waltz" in 1948 (and again in 1951, after Patti Page's multimillion-selling popular version), "Bonaparte's Retreat" (a pop hit for Kay Starr), and the number one hit on both country and pop charts, "Slow Poke," in 1951. At the same time, he had pioneered a television show in Louisville, which eventually grew to a series of regional and national shows in Louisville, Cincinnati, Cleveland, and Chicago, and headlined the ABC Network's *The Pee Wee King Show* for six years. He also found time to appear as musical support in several B westerns through the years.

Gracious and charming, King grew into an ambassador of country music as his performing career wound down. He was elected to the Country Music Hall of Fame in 1974.

As we have seen and will see, few careers flourish without enormous support and contributions by those who may not be as much in the limelight. Therefore no discussion of Pee Wee King can proceed for long

before the name Redd Stewart (1921–2003) comes up. Guitarist, fiddler, smooth vocalist, and songwriter Henry Stewart was born in Tennessee, raised in Kentucky, and joined Pee Wee King in 1937.

A superb, supple singer and a fine musician, he was a songwriter's songwriter; his first success came when Ernest Tubb recorded a tune he co-wrote with King and Tubb called "Soldier's Last Letter" in 1944, which became a number one hit for the Texas Troubadour. Inspired by Bill Monroe's 1946 hit "Kentucky Waltz," he and Pee Wee King wrote "Tennessee Waltz" in the car while on tour; Patti Page's version is reported to have sold nearly five million records. Stewart and King collaborated on several more hits, all of which Stewart sang on their RCA records: "Slow Poke," "Bonaparte's Retreat," "Bimbo." Stewart and King (and WHAS librarian Chilton Price) also wrote "You Belong to Me," which they did not record; however, it was a huge seller for Jo Stafford, and, like the others, has been recorded innumerable times by artists in all genres.

FACING: Pee Wee King, left, and Redd Stewart.

THE WEAPON OF PRAYER

By Ira Louvin and Chas. Louvin

Recorded by LOUVIN BROTHERS for MGM Records

featured by
The Louvin Brothers
Chas. and Ira.

PUBLISHED BY

Acuff-Rose PUBLICATIONS

2510 Franklin Road
NASHVILLE 4, TENNESSEE

MADE IN U.S.A.

The Louvin Brothers

Ira Louvin
(1924–1965)

Charlie Louvin
(1927–   )

The two young Loudermilk boys from rural northern Alabama took the venerable but aging brother duet sound in country music to new levels of creativity and intensity, and though they did not score endless streams of hit records, in their way they have proved to be one of the most influential acts in country music history.

Their mandolin-duet sound, harking back to the heyday of duets in the 1930s, had an archaic quality that was extremely endearing, yet there was a fiery intensity to their singing and great power in their songwriting that hinted at both bluegrass and rockabilly. At the same time, their sacred songs, equally intense and original, have left a mark on that genre as well.

Ira played mandolin, did much of the songwriting, and sang in an unforgettable piercing tenor, which blended beautifully with Charlie's robust smoky baritone. They began appearing on radio as early as 1942, and in 1947 they changed their name to Louvin while at WROL in Knoxville. Their recording career began in a series of fits and starts due to Charlie's call to duty in Korea, and releases on Apollo, Decca, and MGM displayed the traditional yet dynamic mixture that marked their career. Although they recorded, performed, and wrote secular music— their "Are You Teasing Me?" was a hit for Carl Smith in 1951—they were primarily thought of as a sacred act at this stage of their career, and songs like "The Family Who Prays" and "The Christian Life" have become standards in that field.

Their career went into high gear after they signed a publishing contract with Acuff-Rose, and penned a recording contract with Capitol in 1952. Their recorded sound was simple: just the mandolin, rhythm guitar, electric guitar, and bass—not even drums— and those two marvelous voices, which led to several hits in the mid-1950s: "When I Stop Dreaming," "I Don't Believe You've Met My Baby," "Hoping that You're Hoping," "You're Running Wild," "Cash on the Barrel Head," "My Baby's Gone," and, surprisingly, a straightforward version of the venerable folk song "The Knoxville Girl." They became members of the Grand Ole Opry in 1955 as their careers began to soar.

But though they were young and energetic, the rock years took a great toll on their fortunes, as it did most country acts of the time; that and Ira's increasingly unpredictable behavior caused the brothers to formally split in 1963, and both were then signed to Capitol Records as solo artists. It was Charlie who began a run of hit records in the thoroughly contemporary country style of the time, including "I Don't Love You Any More" in 1964 and "See the Big Man Cry" in 1965. He remained on Capitol and on the charts well into the 1970s, and has been a mainstay of the Opry cast ever since.

Ira's solo career and huge creative talent were cut short in a grisly fatal auto accident on a Missouri highway in 1965.

Their music was already a staple of the bluegrass and gospel repertoire; when they were discovered by folk-rockers Gram Parsons and Emmylou Harris (who had a huge hit with their "If I Could Only Win Your Love"), their reputation soared. Their music is more available now than ever, Charles Wolfe has written their fine biography, and they were inducted into the Country Music Hall of Fame in 2001.

Lulu Belle and Scotty

Myrtle Eleanor Cooper Wiseman
(1913–1999)

Scott Wiseman
(1909–1981)

Never big chart hit makers, Lulu Belle and Scotty were affectionately known as America's Country Sweethearts, appeared in more than half a dozen movies, and were the unquestioned stars of the *National Barn Dance* for a quarter of a century.

Lulu Belle, from deep in the mountains in Boone, North Carolina, came to the *National Barn Dance* first: at the age of eighteen this gifted singer and guitarist joined the cast, ostensibly as the girlfriend of the show's headliner, Red Foley. Brash and funny and soulful, she was an immediate hit and, indeed, by 1936 she was voted the "National Radio Queen," the most popular woman on radio. Scott Wiseman, also from the mountains of North Carolina, joined the *Barn Dance* a year later, in 1933, as a folk singer along the lines of Bradley Kincaid, whom he admired deeply. A devoted student of Appalachian folk music (as well as the composer of many folk classics), he was paired with Lulu Belle in 1934 (to the horror of some *National Barn Dance* listeners, who thought her fickle for "leaving" Red Foley), and their make-believe radio romance turned real. They were married in December 1934.

The late 1930s and early 1940s were their heyday, for they were the headliners of the *National Barn Dance*, recorded a couple of dozen successful sides for

Conqueror, Vocalion, and OKeh (mostly in the humorous or sacred vein), and even appeared in half a dozen films, beginning with *Shine On Harvest Moon*, starring Roy Rogers (Republic, 1938), and ending with *Sing, Neighbor, Sing* (Republic, 1944), which featured Roy Acuff and others.

Their charm was their affectionate banter, their close harmony, and the strength of Scotty's songwriting: the most memorable of his many compositions include "Mountain Dew," "Brown Mountain Light," "Remember Me," and the all-time classic "Have I Told You Lately that I Love You?"

Savvy enough to know when their time in the spotlight was over, the couple left the *National Barn Dance* in 1958 and returned to their native western North Carolina. Scotty, though in his middle years, obtained a master's degree and became a teacher, farmer, and bank director. Not to be outdone, Lulu Belle ran for the North Carolina legislature and won two terms. They recorded, in a nostalgic vein, for Starday in the 1960s and Old Homestead in the 1970s, and made limited personal appearances; but for all intents and purposes, they had left their show-business years behind without regret to embrace new opportunities.

Uncle Dave Macon

(1870–1952)

Vernon Dalhart, country music's first recording star, waited until his early forties to begin recording rural tunes, but Uncle Dave Macon waited even longer: he was well into his midfifties when he became country music's first touring and radio star.

A musician from his youth, he absorbed both the folk music of his rolling mid-Tennessee hills and the varied contemporary music of the vaudeville musicians who stayed at his father's

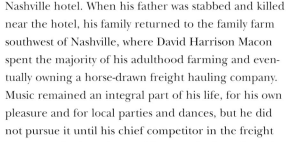

Nashville hotel. When his father was stabbed and killed near the hotel, his family returned to the family farm southwest of Nashville, where David Harrison Macon spent the majority of his adulthood farming and eventually owning a horse-drawn freight hauling company. Music remained an integral part of his life, for his own pleasure and for local parties and dances, but he did not pursue it until his chief competitor in the freight wagon business invested in motorized trucks and quickly put Macon out of business.

A theatrical agent happened to hear Macon and Fiddlin' Sid Harkreader playing old tunes in a Nashville barbershop in 1923 and put the two on tour; they traveled extensively, and by 1925 George D. Hay made Macon one of the first two members of the WSM *Barn Dance*, soon to be known as the *Grand Ole Opry*. Macon also began recording in this heady time, and his wide and

---

LEFT: Uncle Dave Macon, left, strums a banjo.

deep repertoire was captured in his many recordings of the period. Even given his background, the extent of his repertoire is remarkable: folk songs, gospel songs, political and current event songs, comedy, original and political pieces, instrumentals, and blues like "Keep My Skillet Good and Greasy."

He became a staple of the *Grand Ole Opry* radio broadcasts throughout the 1930s, embodying the finest in old-time showmanship. A rare slice of that is captured in the 1940 Republic film *Grand Ole Opry*, where the seventy-year-old Macon stomps his feet and twirls his banjo ("like a monkey handling a peanut") in the finest vaudeville tradition. He remained with the *Grand Ole Opry* right through the war years and the coming of the honky-tonk era, a still-vital holdover from the classic days, right up until his death, at eighty-two, in 1952.

It was obvious then, but even more obvious to us now, that Uncle Dave Macon was a direct link to the tent show and riverboat era of American musical history, a living window into the sounds and styles of the generation preceding Jimmie Rodgers and the Carter Family and Vernon Dalhart. Even today—especially today—his recordings capture the music of an era that blossomed long before the radio and, indeed, before the record player itself.

Bill Monroe

(1911–1996)

Charismatic yet remote, Bill Monroe, his music, and his band, the Blue Grass Boys, named an entire style, a sub-genre of country music. Rather than languishing in obscurity, it is known, studied, played, and enjoyed around the world more so today than ever before. That is quite a stunning legacy for a shy farm boy from western Kentucky.

William Smith Monroe's family, particularly his mother's side, was a musical one, and as the youngest child he was relegated to the mandolin, since brothers Birch and Charlie had already laid claim to the fiddle and guitar, respectively. After spending endless hours learning fiddle tunes from his uncle Pen Vandiver and the blues from guitarist Arthur Shultz, Monroe joined his older brothers near Chicago, where they not only played music but square-danced professionally as well. By 1935 Bill and Charlie had left the refineries and weekend music behind, and pursued their career as the Monroe Brothers in Iowa and Nebraska before hitting their stride on WBT in Charlotte, North Carolina.

Though their first successful Blue Bird record was a moderately paced religious song, "What Would You Give in Exchange for Your Soul?" their music was characterized by a drive and punch that prefigured bluegrass, their harmony soaring and edgy. It wasn't always pretty,

but it was darn sure exciting, and Bill's mandolin work was, for the era, simply brilliant, sparkling above Charlie's strong rhythm guitar. Charlie's voice was high but mellow, while Bill's powerful tenor made for an exciting blend unlike any other of the era, and the pair revitalized the art of the brother duet.

But both were headstrong young men, and despite being at the peak of their success, they parted ways in 1938, Charlie to form Charlie Monroe's Boys, later his Kentucky Partners, while Bill formed his Blue Grass Boys (after his native bluegrass state of Kentucky), and quickly signed to Victor and joined the Grand Ole Opry in 1939. Charlie's fine career went on another decade before his retirement, but Bill's was just taking off, and his early Blue Bird records of "Muleskinner Blues" and "Orange Blossom Special" became big sellers, while the songs themselves became standards of the emerging bluegrass repertoire.

It wasn't quite bluegrass yet, though it was approaching it. Like so many careers on these pages, great success came with the magic of collaboration, and for Monroe, that was adding Lester Flatt on guitar in 1944 and Earl Scruggs on the banjo a few months later. Flatt, who sang in a breezy tenor, recaptured the Monroe Brother's vocal magic, anchoring Monroe's

BILL MONROE'S GRAND OLE OPRY

WSM

SONG FOLIO No. 1

Bill AND HIS HORSE KING WILKIE

2.95
(In U.S.A.)

PEER-SOUTHERN PUBLICATIONS 1740 BROADWAY, NEW YORK, N.Y. 10019

edgy tenor, while Earl Scruggs simply set the country music world on its ear with his revolutionary three-finger banjo style, a sound that virtually defines bluegrass music. This was an exciting band musically as well as vocally, and it established the style as we know it.

Flatt and Scruggs both left in 1948, but not before many of the classic bluegrass songs had been recorded. From then on the Blue Grass Boys became a kind of school for the style, as so many of the next generation of bluegrass performers spent time as Blue Grass Boys, including Jimmy Martin, Don Reno, Mac Wiseman, Sonny Osborne, and Carter Stanley, just a few among dozens. Monroe also had his most popular records in that era, including his top chart record, "Kentucky Waltz" in 1946 and "Footprints in the Snow" the same year, recorded during his association with Columbia Records.

Monroe was always a prolific songwriter, and his songs became more personal, more intense, less optimistic sounding after his move to Decca. Many of them are his true artistic triumphs, and many, particularly "Uncle Pen," are among the core repertoire of the genre today. But as the 1950s progressed, electric instruments and honky-tonk themes pushed his exciting acoustic sound to the rear, and bluegrass, while thriving on a regional basis, seemed in danger of becoming an anachronism.

It was just that anachronistic, archaic feel that appealed to the rapidly expanding audience for folk music in the early 1960s, and their acceptance of Monroe as the die-hard creator and unflinching con-

servator of the style remade his career. Though only in his midfifties at the time, he was recast as the patriarch of a music that quickly found acceptance in suburbs, cities, and campuses across the nation and eventually around the world.

While he may have originally resented bands like Flatt and Scruggs and the Stanley Brothers "copying his style," in the 1960s and 1970s he came to relish his role as the Father of Bluegrass, and attended and promoted bluegrass festivals that now fill summer weekends across the country. Blessed with a hardy pioneer constitution, he continued to record and tour and play at the Grand Ole Opry until well into his eighties, before suffering the stroke that eventually took his life in 1996.

Patsy Montana

(1908–1996)

Patsy Montana parlayed a sweet smile, sparkling eyes, and the ability to yodel into an honor-filled career that lasted more than sixty years. She has long been celebrated for having recorded country music's first hit record by a woman, "I Want to Be a Cowboy's Sweetheart," in 1935.

Born Ruby Blevins in Hot Springs, Arkansas, the eleventh child of a subsistence farmer, she grew up in Hope, Arkansas, and attended college in Louisiana She headed for California in about 1930, where she met with the extremely popular Stuart Hamblen and took the name Patsy Montana. A return visit to Arkansas brought her to station KWKH in Shreveport, Louisiana, where she met Jimmie Davis, who took her to New Jersey to record with him in 1932, accompanying him on some tracks and recording her own sides for Victor as well.

She chanced to meet the Kentucky Ramblers, a popular new string band, while visiting the Century of Progress World's Fair in 1933 and was asked to join the band: they were a string band in search of a singer, she a singer in search of a band. Reflecting the rising national interest in western music, and because they were stars of WLS in Chicago (Illinois being the Prairie State), they changed their name to the Prairie Ramblers. It was as Patsy Montana and the Prairie Ramblers that she recorded "I Want to Be a Cowboy's Sweetheart."

Though she never had another hit like it, she recorded frequently the next few years and became one of the most popular acts on the *National Barn Dance*, and even sang "Cowboy's Sweetheart" in a Gene Autry film in 1939. Her sunny personality and sparkling yodeling were featured on Decca records after 1940, when she left the Prairie Ramblers. She hosted her own network radio show, *Wake Up And Smile*,

LEFT: Patsy Montana and the Prairie Ramblers: Chick Hurt, left, Tex Atchison, Jack Taylor, and Salty Holmes.

over ABC in 1946 and 1947.

With two young girls to raise and changing tastes in the music business, she and her husband and children left Chicago and moved to Arkansas for a time, where she continued to appear on local radio and on the *Louisiana Hayride* in Shreveport. However, show business was in her blood, and the family then immigrated to California where, in grand show business tradition, her daughters were brought into the act.

Rock and roll and the decline of western and traditional country music looked like it might have drawn the curtain on her career, but Montana was resilient and loved to perform. She found a whole new home in folk music, where her music was seen as proto-feminist, and in Europe, where traditional country music was still accepted and even treasured.

Patsy Montana continued to perform at folk and bluegrass festivals and to tour Europe well into the 1990s, a second career that she embraced wholeheartedly. Her endless energy, unfailing good humor, refreshing humility, and charming yodeling won over a whole new generation and kept her busy right up until her death. It was just as she wanted it. She was elected to the Country Music Hall of Fame in 1996, just months after her death.

For Marian Campbull
with Best Wishes!
Minnie Pearl

MINNIE PEARL

**W.S.M.
GRAND OLE OPRY**

Minnie Pearl

(1912–1996)

Minnie Pearl was the face of country culture and music to a host of Americans who otherwise ignored it or didn't care for it in an era when the music was coming to national consciousness. She was a deeply loved ambassador throughout her entire career. Although not a musician or singer (though she did both as part of her act, exaggerating her musical shortcomings), her larger-than-life character of the gossipy, man-hungry small-town girl with the price tag on her hat and the brazen "How-dee!" touched something in many Americans beyond her region and made her a national figure in a way she could not have done as a singer.

Born Sarah Ophelia Colley to a well-to-do family in Centerville, Tennessee, she aspired to become an actress and, after graduating from college, went on the road with the Wayne P. Sewell Production Company. It was on these tours that young Sarah Colley, inspired by several of the small-town women she met, developed the Minnie Pearl character, which she debuted at a women's club function in 1940. Executives at WSM heard about this character by chance, and in November 1940 she debuted on the Grand Ole Opry and was almost immediately made a cast member.

When the Opry went on the NBC network in 1942 with the *Prince Albert Show*, she became one of its stars; it was on this show she developed the raucous "How-dee!" that became her trademark.

Minnie Pearl made the most of her sudden stardom, and while she appeared on the *Grand Ole Opry* for five decades, she also became a familiar sight on television in the 1950s, with appearances on Tennessee Ernie Ford's and Dinah Shore's network programs, as well as the *Tonight Show*, the 1960s saw her expand her appearances to Carol Burnett's and Jonathan Winters' shows.

Meanwhile, back at the Opry she teamed with Rod Brasfield; their special magic produced a great number of her best routines, and the partnership lasted until Brasfield's death in 1958. As the years rolled on she became a cast member of *Hee Haw*, both on the network and in syndication, and was a frequent guest on the Nashville Network as it became a presence in cable television.

She recorded a bit, mostly comedic bits—although the extremely atypical, tear-jerking "Giddyup Go—Answer" became a surprise top-ten hit in 1966—and continued to perform well into the 1990s, often with Roy Acuff as her foil. Though she professed to want to return to the limelight, a 1991 stroke ended her career, and country music lost one of its most vivid and recognizable family members when she finally passed away in 1996. She was elected to the Country Music Hall of Fame in 1975.

Webb Pierce

(1921–1991)

Some artists' reputations, for whatever reason, do not seem to thrive after they are gone, and Webb Pierce is certainly the prime example of that unhappy phenomenon. While his contemporaries Lefty Frizzell and Hank Williams have been revered and profoundly influential, Pierce's star has faded into near obscurity despite his astonishing track record of thirteen number one singles and ninety-six chart records.

Perhaps it is the unrelenting, brassy tenor voice with the tight vibrato that resonates poorly with today's audience; perhaps it's because he was too much a man of his era, a honky-tonker's honky-tonker, far removed from contemporary sounds and styles. Regardless, he is doubtless due a revival, for in his day he shone with the brightest.

He was born Webb Michael Pierce in West Monroe, Louisiana, and grew up on western swing. He once stated, matter-of-factly, that since everyone seemed to be trying to sing in a sun-warmed baritone like Bob Wills' longtime singer Tommy Duncan, he began singing at the top of his range to set himself apart from the rest, developing his unique attack and style. After service in World War II he moved to Shreveport, Louisiana, and there worked for years trying to get on radio and records. It took a little while; his sound was very different, but a position on the *Louisiana Hayride* and some independent label recording led to his first major label contract in 1951, with Decca.

It was magic from the start. "Wondering," went to number one in 1952, and his following two singles—

"That Heart Belongs to Me" and "Back Street Affair"—also hit the top spot that year. Though that could not go on forever, of course, still the hits followed, including honky-tonk classics like "It's Been So Long," "There Stands the Glass," "Even Tho," "More and More," "I Don't Care," "Love, Love, Love," and "Slowly," which, thanks to musician Bud Isaacs, introduced the pedal steel guitar to country music.

Pierce joined the Grand Ole Opry in 1952 but left during its upheaval in the mid-1950s; he also appeared frequently on the televised *Ozark Jubilee* in his heyday.

The rock-and-roll years, cruel to all country entertainers, were difficult for Pierce, although he continued to rack up top-ten records on the country charts, including such classics as "Walking the Dog," "Tupelo County Jail," "No Love Have I," and his only pop crossover hit, the strange "I Ain't Never," in 1959. Although he continued to chart records regularly even into the early 1970s, he didn't fit in with either the rock-tinged country or the smooth countrypolitan Nashville Sound, and, as always, remained something of a musical outsider, always going his own way.

Webb Pierce had invested well in publishing and several other businesses, and had little need by that time to tour much or record. He was far better known for bus tours of his mansion with its guitar-shaped swimming pool (as well as his rhinestone spangled

Webb
PIERCE

For Bookings: 146 7th Avenue, N., Nashville
Country Music — 10 — Who's Who

Nudie suits and his silver-dollar encrusted Pontiac) by the time he made his final recording, with Willie Nelson, in 1982. His final years were quiet ones, and he died of pancreatic cancer in 1991. He was elected, at last, to the Country Music Hall of Fame in 2001.

Ray Price

(1926 –   )

Not unlike Eddy Arnold, Ray Noble Price entirely recast his career in the 1960s and 1970s, and became a hit maker of legendary proportions twice over.

Born near Perryville, Texas, Price was attending veterinary school and singing at local honky-tonks when he was discovered by Jim Beck and recorded two sides for Bullett Records before signing with Columbia in 1951. His early records, like many of the era, were much in the mold of the incandescent Hank Williams, with whom Price shared a house during 1952, the same year he joined the Grand Ole Opry. He broke out with his own sound and style in 1954 with two songs that, like so much of his repertoire, have become timeless country classics: "I'll Be There," and "Release Me."

From there he developed the classic country shuffle that defined his early success and created a genre of country music that for years was identified as "the Ray Price sound," typified by his first number one hit, "Crazy Arms," in 1956, which featured his unique vocals, a soaring tenor harmony, a prominent, dipsy doodle fiddle line, and that infectious shuffle beat provided by his Cherokee Cowboys. The following years brought hit after hit in that style, and many of the songs became staples of the shuffle genre: "My Shoes Keep Walking Back to You" in 1957, "City Lights" and "Invitation to the Blues" in 1958, "Heartaches by the Number" and "Under Your Spell Again" in 1959, "One More Time" in 1960, "Heart Over Mind" in 1961, and "Pride" in 1962.

But even this early, Price felt the winds of change and began to adapt. While he still had hits in the classic shuffle style—like "Burning Memories" in 1964, "The Other Woman" in 1965, and "Touch My Heart" in 1966—as early as 1962 he began recording ballads like "Make the World Go Away," a trend that culminated with his full orchestral version of "Danny Boy" in 1967. The shift was dramatic—though not at all pleasing to country music traditionalists of the era—and resulted in a string of huge hit records, pop and country, which included "For the Good Times," "I Won't Mention It Again," "She's Got to Be a Saint," and "You're the Best Thing that Ever Happened to Me" in the early 1970s.

While not as musically influential as his shuffle period, this era was by far his most commercially successful, and though he charted records well into the late 1980s, a remake of "Faded Love" in 1980 was his last top-ten record. Dropped by Columbia in 1974, he left Nashville in disillusionment and returned to Texas, where he continues an active and productive road career unabated, and, at this writing, still tours and has a commanding stage presence and voice at the age of eighty-two. Ray Price was elected to the Country Music Hall of Fame in 1996, an honor long overdue for this trendsetter and hit maker in two diverse and equally influential country music styles.

Riley Puckett

(1894–1946)

One of country music's true pioneers, Riley Puckett was there at the creation, recording frequently and influentially from the very infancy of the country music recording industry right up until the dawn of the Second World War.

Born near Alpharetta, Georgia, Puckett was virtually blinded as a youth, and it was at the Macon School for the Blind that he began playing the banjo and guitar as a teenager. His playing could be eccentric, even bizarre, but his singing was smooth, distinctive, and powerful. His career as a professional musician flourished at dances long before he went on WSB in Atlanta in 1922 in the fledgling days of radio.

In addition to his lengthy career as a vocalist, he was also in demand as a musician in a string band setting, and in the early 1920s, when recording companies stumbled upon the huge untapped market for country music, Puckett was one of the earliest and most prolific performers; indeed, only Vernon Dalhart sold more records in that pre-Depression era. Puckett recorded on his own as early as 1924, accompanied by rough-hewn but charismatic fiddler Gid Tanner, with whom he formed the Skillet Lickers string band, which recorded prolifically throughout the 1920s.

Puckett's repertoire was all over the place. Unfettered by musical boundaries real or imagined, he

LEFT: Riley Puckett, left, and Gid Tanner.

Photos courtesy of Country Music Hall of Fame® and Museum.

not to Puckett's career. He record-ed and performed with country swing fiddler (and Skillet Licker alumnus) Clayton McMichen and his Georgia Wildcats, with a re-formed version of the Skillet Lickers, as well as in dozens of solo and duet settings. Columbia had folded in the early days of the Depression, so Puckett did not record again on his own until landing with Blue Bird from 1934 to 1936, then Decca in 1937, and again on Blue Bird from 1939 to 1941. Once again, the wide vari-ety of songs is astonishing, mixing western ("South of the Border," "Back on the Texas Plains"), pure pop ("Ma, He's Making Eyes at Me," "Oh, Johnny, Oh"), coun-try ("When It's Peach Picking Time in Georgia"), novelty ("The Story of the Preacher and the Bear"), sentimental ("Old Fashioned Locket"), and Irish ("When Irish Eyes Are Smiling").

Puckett didn't record after 1941 but was as active as ever with touring and on the radio, appearing with the Stone Mountain Boys in Atlanta at the time of his death, which was as unusual as his life had been: an untreated boil on his neck led to blood poisoning, and he died in an Atlanta hospital at the age of fifty-two.

recorded string band breakdowns, sentimental songs, folk songs, yodels, blues, pop songs, Hawaiian, cowboy, Irish—well, you name it, he did it—and was Columbia Records' major country recording artist.

The Depression put an end to these heady days but

Jim Reeves

(1923–1964)

The poster boy for the ultra-slick Nashville Sound of the 1960s, James Travis Reeves had a solid career in traditional country music that ensured his lasting legacy before the flood of countrypolitan hits.

Born in Galloway, Texas, in Panola County—the same East Texas county that nurtured Tex Ritter—Reeves grew up with twin loves of music and baseball. He attended the University of Texas on a baseball scholarship but dropped out to enter the service during World War II. He failed his physical, so he became a welder, and then went into professional baseball before an injury ended that dream.

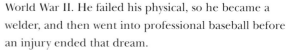

His rich, smooth voice was a natural for radio, and he continued to sing with local bands while working as a disc jockey at several small stations in Texas. He recorded several promising singles for the Macy's label in 1949, and then moved up to upstart Abbott records in 1952, where "Mexican Joe" became his first bona fide hit. It brought him to the *Louisiana Hayride* as both announcer and performer, and scored him another hit record, "Bimbo," in 1953.

As with many performers, a spot on the *Louisiana Hayride* led to an offer from the Grand Ole Opry, and he not only joined the cast but signed a recording contract with RCA in 1955 as well.

He got off to a strong start with a top-ten hit, "Yonder Comes a Sucker," in 1955, the first of some forty hit singles, which took on a glossier, violin-textured sound with "Am I Losing You?" and "Four Walls," a number one record in 1957. Other hits in the new style followed: "Anna Marie" and "Blue Boy" in 1958,

"Billy Bayou" in 1959, and the huge crossover hit, "He'll Have to Go," in 1960. His mellow baritone proved popular among record buyers at home, and he became a very successful artist overseas as well, going so far as to star in a South African film, *Kimberly Jim.*

The hits kept coming, including "The Blizzard" in 1961, "Adios Amigo" in 1962, "Welcome to My World" and "I Guess I'm Crazy," both in 1964. However, at his artistic and professional peak, Reeves and his manager were killed in the crash of his private plane just outside Nashville.

He cast a long shadow, however, and RCA continued to release posthumous singles, several of which went to number one on the charts, including "This Is It" and "Is It Really Over?" in 1965, "Distant Drums" and "The Blue Side of Lonesome" in 1966, and "I Won't Come in While He's There" in 1967. Indeed, repackaged albums continued to appear, and the singles kept coming: the late Reeves had singles on the charts every year up until 1984,

when RCA finally ran out of available tracks to release or repackage.

Originally a traditional country singer, Reeves was a pioneer in creating a whole new sound for an industry that was struggling to stay afloat during the rock-and-roll years, and his expressive baritone was the perfect match for the sweeping string arrangements of the new Nashville Sound. He was elected to the Country Music Hall of Fame in 1967.

TEX RITTER IN

Tex Ritter

(1905–1974)

Though his image and success as a singing cowboy film star has tended to obscure it, Tex Ritter also had a long and extremely successful career in country music, particularly as a record seller.

Born Woodward (which he and his family pronounced Wood'ard) Maurice Ritter in Panola County in East Texas, he was both musical and bright as a child. He worked his way through the University of Texas as a radio singer of cowboy songs in the 1920s; it was at UT that he was mentored by folklorists and folk song scholars J. Frank Dobie, Oscar J. Fox, and John Lomax, who fueled the fire of Ritter's passion for traditional cowboy folk songs. Indeed, Tex Ritter was by far the most knowledgeable and authoritative of the singing cowboys on cowboy folk songs and their origins.

But the show business bug had bitten hard, and while attending law school at UT, he basically ran off with a touring New York production. When that show closed, he stayed in New York, where he quickly developed a fine career on Broadway, with his most notable role in *Green Grow the Lilacs*. He also began recording as early as 1932 and became popular on radio as a singer and actor on several shows (where he became known as Tex), and as a co-host of New York's answer to the *Grand Ole Opry*, the WHN *Barn Dance*.

It was on that show that he was discovered by up-and-coming film executive Edward Finney, who signed Ritter to a contract and brought him to Hollywood, where Gene Autry's films were creating a demand for singing cowboys. With his deep knowledge of western song and folklore, his non-pretty-boy good looks, his acting experience, and especially his distinctive, instantly recognizable voice, he seemed like a natural. He quickly became one of America's top cowboy stars, though he often toiled for second-rate studios like Grand National, Monogram, and PRC in his ten-year film career, as well as for larger B studios Universal and Columbia. He ultimately made some eighty-five westerns as a singing cowboy.

Ritter had recorded for nearly a decade for the ARC complex of labels and for Decca, largely in the western vein, before signing with the brand-new Capitol label in 1942, where he had his first bona fide hit, "Jingle, Jangle, Jingle." Switching over to pure

FACING: Tex Ritter and Evelyn Finley in *Arizona Troutier* (Monogram, 1940).

country love songs, he had an astonishing string of hits in the war years, including "I'm Wasting My Tears on You" and "There's a New Moon Over My Shoulder" in 1944, and "Jealous Heart," "You Will Have to Pay," and "You Two-Timed Me One Time Too Often" in 1945. His association with Capitol lasted until his death, and he recorded dozens of albums of wildly divergent types, from cowboy folk songs to orchestral jazz to Spanish language to spoken word to children's music to patriotic to religious to contemporary country. In addition, his voice graced the soundtrack of the classic film *High Noon*, which also became a hit record for him in 1952.

An inveterate, almost compulsive tourer, Ritter crisscrossed America for the rest of his life and continued to rack up popular records as the decades passed, most notably "The Wayward Wind" in 1956 and "I Dreamed of a Hillbilly Heaven" in 1961. It was one of the many recitations with which he found great success late in his career. One of the founders of the Country Music Association, and one of its early presidents, Ritter eventually moved to Nashville in 1965 to join the Grand Ole Opry, to co-host a show on WSM radio, and to continue touring with a country band. Although he took a little time out to run an unsuccessful campaign for the U.S. Senate in 1970, he was still touring at the time of his sudden death, of heart failure, in 1974.

He was an original, one of a kind. He was the rare combination of entertainer and scholar, a far better actor than he generally had the chance to show, a major record seller, and a film star. His voice was like no other: unique and instantly recognizable. He was elected to the Country Music Hall of Fame in 1964.

Marty Robbins

(1925–1982)

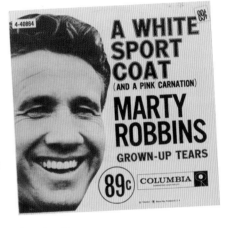

Though the large portion of his success came after the somewhat arbitrary 1955 cutoff date of the artists included in this volume, Marty Robbins' star shone so brightly in the early years of his long career that he demands inclusion. He was a star from the start. That he would become a superstar is no surprise. That he was able to achieve success in so very many country music genres remains a feat unequaled.

Born in Glendale, Arizona, Martin David Robinson obtained his own radio and television shows in Phoenix in 1947, after having served in the Pacific with the navy in World War II. A guest on his TV show, Little Jimmy Dickens, brought him to the attention of the Grand Ole Opry and Dickens' record label; Marty Robbins signed with both in 1952. He not only became a favorite on the show with his showmanship, soaring voice, and youthful good looks, but also rewarded Columbia with a number one hit, "I'll Go on Alone," right off the bat in December 1952.

He was often billed as "Mister Teardrop" for the sad ballads and the catch in his voice, but in mid-decade he found great success covering rockabilly songs for the country market, leading to his second number one, "Singing the Blues," in 1956, quickly followed by "A White Sport Coat (and a Pink Carnation)" and "The Story of My Life" in 1957, and "Just Married" in 1958.

Deeply influenced by the songwriting of Bob Nolan and the music of the Sons of the Pioneers as a youth, he welcomed the chance to sing and record the title song to the film *The Hanging Tree* in 1959, and this rekindled his love of western music; his own song "El Paso" went to number one in 1959 and led to a series of best-selling albums of western music. At the same time he also explored Hawaiian music, to which his beautiful falsetto was perfectly suited.

More crossover pop/country hits followed in quick succession: "Don't Worry" in 1961, "Devil Woman" (now exploring Caribbean/calypso) and "Ruby Ann" in 1962, "Begging to You" in 1963. In the 1960s he began embracing the art of the pop ballad and racked up several more number one hits: "Ribbon of Darkness" in 1965, "I Walk Alone" in 1968, and "My Woman, My Woman, My Wife" in 1970. Although he remained on the charts until his untimely death, his last number one records were "El Paso City" and "Among My Souvenirs" in 1976. This astonishing list covers only his number one hits. Other top-ten records included such classics as "I Couldn't Keep from Crying," "That's All Right," "Knee Deep in the Blues," "Big Iron," "The Cowboy in the Continental Suit," and "Love Me," a handful among many. He appeared in several films (some of them westerns), did syndicated and network television as well during the 1960s and 1970s, and became an avid stock car racer, living every minute of his life fully.

As both a singer and a songwriter he was comfortable in an extremely wide variety of country-oriented genres, and his charm and availability to his fans was legendary. However, his heart was flawed, and in 1969 he suffered his first heart attack, underwent then-experimental bypass surgery, and survived more than a dozen years more before succumbing to heart failure at the age of fifty-seven. He was inducted into the Country Music Hall of Fame in 1982, just two months before his untimely death.

Carson J. Robison

(1890–1957)

Of all the artists profiled on these pages whose careers can be said to have been unjustly allowed to slip into obscurity, none have suffered worse than Carson J. Robison. Like his erstwhile singing partner Vernon Dalhart, his frequent success with the popular music of the time and his longtime residence in New York have perhaps branded him as a city-billy of sorts. Yet, like Dalhart, his country background is impeccable. He has not been inducted into the Country Music Hall of Fame, nor does his name spring to the tongue when the great pioneers of the style are mentioned, yet his contributions to the early years of country music were more than substantial, and he deserves to be well remembered.

Born to a musical family in Oswego, Kansas, he decided after serving in World War I that music was his true calling. He moved to Kansas City in 1920, becoming part of the burgeoning jazz scene there, though his first appearance on the radio was as a cowboy singer in 1922. He became associated with one-hit-wonder Wendell Hall ("It Ain't Gonna Rain No Mo'") and, figuring his future was in the music capital of New York, moved there in 1924, where he found immediate work in the heart of the jazz age as a whistler, guitarist,

singer, and songwriter. Within months of arriving in New York, he teamed up with Dalhart, with whom he recorded as a guitarist and tenor singer, and for whom he wrote songs exclusively.

Dalhart's recording output became so prodigious he found he needed an inexhaustible source of material, and that source was Robison, who could churn out songs as fast as Dalhart could record them. Robison's specialty was event and disaster songs, so popular in that era, and his subjects included train wrecks, Charles Lindbergh's transatlantic flight, and the Scopes trial, among many others. Other compositions, many of which would become country standards, included "Little Green Valley," "Left My Gal in the Mountains," "Open Up Them Pearly Gates," "Carry Me Back to the Lone Prairie," "New River Train," "Sleepy Rio Grande," and scores of others.

However, this arrangement, so beneficial to both, resulted in a rancorous split when Dalhart demanded an increasingly bigger share of Robison's songwriting royalties, feeling the songs were selling so well because Dalhart was recording them. When Dalhart's demands grew too high, Robison, figuring the records were selling so well because Robison was writing them, terminated the partnership. Unwilling to go solo, he immediately found another partner, Frank Luther, and they inaugurated a series of hit records—very much in the Dalhart-Robison Style—with a national best seller "Barnacle Bill the Sailor" (another Robison composition) in 1929. They recorded nearly three hundred songs together before an amicable parting in 1932.

Sensing the growing national interest in cowboy and western songs, he then concentrated on writing and performing romantic pictorial songs of the West rather than the mountain or current event songs that had been his staple, and put together a group he first called Carson Robison and his Pioneers, and later called Carson Robison and his Buckaroos. This was the first country or western band to tour overseas; he took this troupe to England, Australia, and New Zealand in 1932, and returned to England again in 1936 and 1939. He continued to record and had a network

radio show as well during the 1930s, and reinvented himself once again during the war years by reverting to the current events song, scoring a big wartime anti-Hitler hit called "1942 Turkey in the Straw."

Indefatigable and irrepressible, he had one final hit in 1948 at the age of fifty-eight: the drawling, laconic, tongue-in-cheek "Life Gets Tee-just, Don't It" for the brand-new MGM label. Following that he more or less retired to his Duchess County estate in upstate New York and died just as the craze for folk music was beginning, a craze that celebrated some of his music, and was not entirely dissimilar to the one he helped create and shape some forty years earlier.

Jimmie Rodgers

(1897–1933)

The father of country music was not, at first glance, made of the stuff of stardom: slender, stooped, and swarthy, with a crooked grin and a way of singing out of the side of his mouth, he was hardly the model one would have picked for stardom. Much of his material, too, went counter to the grain: in an era where country music was positioning itself as the music of nostalgia, with barn dance fiddle bands and sentimental singers, Jimmie Rodgers proudly proclaimed himself as a rambler and a rounder, and unashamedly brought in strong influences of the blues from his native Mississippi, in vivid contrast to the stark Appalachian sounds of many of his contemporaries.

Rodgers's mother, a cultivated woman with degrees in English and music, introduced him to a wide variety of musical styles when he was young. But James Charles Rodgers was an unruly youngster, and more or less ran wild when he went to live with his father in 1911. Already a performer, as a teen he ran away with a tent show, and then a medicine show, but he eventually settled down to workaday life, joining his father as a railroad laborer.

Laid off in 1920, the newly married youngster alternated day labor with fitful tours and musical sojourns, but by 1924 he was diagnosed with the tuberculosis that would eventually kill him. He went back to railroading a couple more times but grew so weak he could no longer perform the labor. He migrated as far west as Tucson and as far east as Asheville, North Carolina, before ending up in Johnson City, Tennessee, where he became part of the popular Tenneva Ramblers string band, which was among the several bands (including the Carter Family) that were to record for Ralph Peer on his famous field trip to Bristol in August 1927. An argument over what to officially call the band on the record on the eve of the recording sessions led to the Tenneva Ramblers recording their own selection of tunes, while the irascible Rodgers sang solo, with just his guitar for accompaniment.

The songs, "The Soldier's Sweetheart" and "Sleep, Baby, Sleep," were successful enough that Rodgers was invited back for a second session in November 1927. It was there he recorded "Blue Yodel" (the song we now think of commonly as "T For Texas"), which immediately became a huge hit. The public was entranced by the mournful yodel, the drawling adenoidal voice with the thick Mississippi accent, and haunting and revolutionary mixing of black and white musical styles.

He was quick to return to the studio, and he recorded an eclectic mixture of songs: sentimental, railroad, vaudeville, cowboy, and, of course, a long series of blue yodels. Some of the most familiar include "Waiting for a Train," "In the Jailhouse Now," "Way Out on the Mountain," "Brakeman's Blues," "Hobo Bill's Last Ride," and "Miss the Mississippi and You." By the following year he was a major star, touring the top vaudeville houses, appearing on radio, and selling millions of records.

However, the disease continued to ravage his weakened body. He knew, in the words of one of his painfully autobiographical songs, that "My Time Ain't Long." He lived life to the hilt, actively touring and recording (despite the crushing blow the Depression gave to his concert ticket sales and record sales), and, indeed, he was recording up until the last days of his life, resting on a cot between takes.

Easily the most influential performer in this volume, Rodgers had immediate impact on the next generation of performers, who were mesmerized by his records: Ernest Tubb, Hank Snow, Bill Monroe, Roy Rogers, Grandpa Jones, and many others, especially Gene Autry. These went on to influence hundreds of other performers in their turn, from Eddy Arnold to Lefty Frizzell to Hank Williams to Merle Haggard, and so many more who kept alive, in concert and on record, a taste of

the lonesome, infectious, groundbreaking sound of the Singing Brakeman, Jimmie Rodgers. He was the first performer (with Fred Rose and Hank Williams) elected to the Country Music Hall of Fame in 1961.

The Singing Brakeman

Carl Smith
(1927–   )

Smith is one of several of the bright young stars who brought a sharper edge to country music in the early 1950s, his hard country sound—which featured drums, electric guitar, and the crying steel guitar of Johnny Sibert—was distinctive and unique, as was his deep country baritone. Born in Maynardville, Tennessee, Smith grew up idolizing hometown hero Roy Acuff. After high school and a stint in the navy, he went on to play bass with bands headed by Skeets Williamson and Molly O'Day at WROL in Knoxville.

His singing talents were uncovered, an acetate was sent to WSM in Nashville, and he was brought over to join the Grand Ole Opry in 1950. He signed with Columbia Records in short order, and both were rewarded handsomely with three chart-topping records in 1951: "Let's Live a Little" a remarkable first release that went to number two, and then "Mr. Moon" and "If Teardrops Were Pennies," both of which went to number one. "Let Old Mother Nature Have Her Way" rounded out his magic year of 1951, but Smith remained a significant presence on the charts, racking up some thirty-one top-ten singles in the course of the decade, among them "(When You Feel Like You're In Love) Don't Just Stand There," "Are You Teasing Me?" and "It's a Lovely Lovely World" in 1952; "Hey Joe" in 1953; "Loose Talk" and "Back Up Buddy" in 1954; "Kisses Don't Lie" in 1955; "Why

Why" in 1957; and "Ten Thousand Drums" in 1959, his last top-ten record.

It was a busy decade for the young man: in addition to touring he made a couple of cheapie westerns; he and June Carter married and divorced. (Their daughter Carlene had a fine run on the country charts as a performer in recent years.) He then married another popular performer, Goldie Hill, and this union lasted until her death in 2005. Having appeared frequently on Red Foley's *Ozark Jubilee* television show, he became one of the hosts of its follow-up, ABC's country music television series *Five Star Jubilee*.

Smith remained a presence on the charts, on the road, and on television, having filmed 190 episodes of a network show in Canada, *Carl Smith's Country Music Hall*, which was also syndicated in the U.S., for a number of years. He showed vocal and musical versatility in later years, recording western swing and even a bluegrass album; his hard-edged voice worked well in both genres.

Carl Smith had invested well and was as passionate about raising horses on his Franklin, Tennessee, ranch as he was about music. He chose to bow gracefully out of the performing limelight in 1979 and settle into the life of a gentleman rancher and horse breeder, a life he enjoys to this day. He was inducted into the Country Music Hall of Fame in 2003.

EXCLUSIVE
CARL SMITH
STORY
TOLD IN SONG, PICTURES,
AUTOBIOGRAPHY

COLUMBIA
RECORDING ARTIST

Hank Snow

(1914 – 1999)

In an era of distinctive stylists, when an artist could be identified within seconds of turning on the radio, Hank Snow was truly a stylist's stylist. His clipped enunciation, drawling adenoidal baritone, and aggressive yet tasty acoustic guitar solos made him one of the most distinctive artists in country music history.

Born in Brooklyn, Nova Scotia, Clarence Eugene Snow was a small child who sought escape from abuse and poverty with the help of a guitar and the music of Jimmie Rodgers. Barely into his twenties, he obtained a radio show in Halifax and then a contract with RCA Victor of Canada in 1936, and his career blossomed.

A move to the United States seemed inevitable, and by 1944 he was a member of the Wheeling Jamboree. He and his trick pony Shawnee even tried Hollywood briefly, but it was at the Big D Jamboree in Dallas that he was invited by Ernest Tubb, a fellow Jimmie Rodgers acolyte, to guest on the Grand Ole Opry. Snow's distinctive style and charismatic stage presence convinced the powers that be to confer membership on him in 1950.

Although his U.S. record releases had met with only lukewarm success, that changed abruptly when "I'm Moving On" became a national hit in 1950, spending a full twenty-one weeks at number one. It was the

first of a string of hits that made Snow one of country music's top stars of the early 1950s: "Rumba Boogie," "The Golden Rocket," "Bluebird Island" (with Anita

Carter), "A Tangled Mind," and "I Don't Hurt Anymore." Snow charted a remarkable twenty-four top-ten hits between 1951 and 1955, and continued to be a steady record seller and touring artist during the rock-and-roll years.

Hank Snow continued to have hits well into the early 1960s, including "Miller's Cave" in 1960, "I've Been Everywhere" in 1962, and "Ninety Miles an Hour (Down a Dead End Street)" in 1963. Though the hits slowed down as the countrypolitan sound swept country music, Snow pulled off the remarkable feat of becoming the oldest country artist to have a number one record, when he scored with "Hello Love" in 1974, at the age of sixty-one.

His hit record days were over after that, but his career stayed steady and strong, divided between road work and his growing status as one of the legends of the Grand Ole Opry. When he was dropped by RCA in 1981, it marked another accomplishment that may never be equaled: forty-seven years with the same record company.

Hank Snow's final years were devoted primarily to Grand Ole Opry appearances, to writing an autobiography, and to working with his Hank Snow Foundation for Child Abuse. He appeared regularly on the Opry into his eighties, still strong of voice and sure-handed on his Martin guitar. Hank Snow was inducted into the Country Music Hall of Fame in 1979, one of the most colorful and distinctive artists in country music history.

HANK SNOW *The Singing Ranger*
America's Newest Recording Star

$1.50

Reg. U. S. Pat. Off.
HILL AND RANGE SONGS, INC.
1619 BROADWAY, NEW YORK 19, N.Y.

HANK'S favorite Songs
the Yodeling Ranger

ARRANGED FOR
VOICE, PIANO
VIOLIN
OR GUITAR

PRICE 60 CENTS

Mills Music, Inc.

BOB NOLAN • TIM SPENCER • HUGH FARR • KARL FARR • LLOYD PERRYMAN • PAT BRADY

Bob Nolan and the

Sons of the Pioneers

TOP WESTERN SINGING ORGANIZATION

—SCREEN—
Republic Pictures

—RADIO—
"Roy Rogers Show" N.B.C.
For Alka-Seltzer

—RODEOS—
The ROHR Company
"Roy Rogers Rodeos"

—RECORDINGS—
R.C.A. Victor

Exclusive Management MONTER-GRAY, INC., 8736 Sunset Blvd., Hollywood, Calif.

Sons of the Pioneers

(1933 –)

The Sons of the Pioneers have always written and included country music in their repertoire, and country music has always embraced their songs and style as one of its many branches. Yet they, more than any other person or group, set the sound and the style, as well as the high musical standards, of the music we think of as western today.

The outfit was formed in the musically fertile Southern California of the Depression era by three young veterans of a handful of short- and long-lived country and cowboy bands. Chief among them was Len Slye, an Ohio transplant with a beautiful solo voice and the ability to perform stunning trick yodels. Vern (later better known as Tim) Spencer was a Missouri transplant who sang well, yodeled a bit, had a great head for business, and wrote some of the most enduring western songs of all time. Bob Nolan, a Canadian, was the dreamer and visionary of the group, had a distinctive baritone voice, and was so brilliant as a songwriter he became known as the Stephen Foster of the twentieth century.

They called themselves the Pioneer Trio; a radio announcer, declaring them too young to be Pioneers, introduced them as the Sons of the Pioneers one day, and the name stuck. They were soon joined by fiddler and bass singer Hugh Farr, who, since none of the others were instrumental virtuosos, soon brought his jazz guitarist brother Karl into the band.

Their sound was so original, their harmony so tight, their original songs so vivid and evocative of the West, that they quickly began recording, doing personal appearances, and playing on the radio. They found their way into films in the then brand-new singing cowboy genre with Charles Starrett, Dick Foran, and Gene Autry, who made one of Nolan's songs, "Tumbling Tumbleweeds," the title of a Republic movie and a million-selling record as well.

Spencer left the group in 1936 and was replaced by nineteen-year-old Lloyd Perryman, a strong guitarist with a lyric tenor voice; at this point the sound truly coalesced, and the list of original songs they produced in this era virtually forms the body of essential western music: "Timber Trail," "Blue Prairie," "Chant of the Wanderer," "Cool Water," "The Everlasting Hills of Oklahoma," and dozens of others—all written by Nolan or Spencer or, occasionally, both—came out of this period.

Spencer returned to the group when Len Slye landed a contract as a film star at Republic under the name of Roy Rogers, and Pat Brady joined the group as bassist at that point as well. The boys could not have been busier for the next few years, cranking out eight or more Charles Starrett westerns a year for Columbia and touring between times. When their contract with Columbia was up in 1941 they joined their old saddle pal Roy Rogers at Republic, where they remained until 1947. In addition, they recorded extensively for ARC, Decca, and RCA. Perryman and Brady were replaced by Ken Carson and Shug Fisher, respectively, while they served overseas in the Second World War; both men would make many contributions to the pioneer sound, and Fisher returned to the group a couple of times.

Their movie career dwindled in the late 1940s, but they achieved a good deal of recording success on the country charts in that era with hits like "No One to Cry to," "Baby Doll," new versions of "Tumbling Tumbleweeds" and "Cool Water," "Teardrops in My Heart," and Spencer's perennial classic "Room Full of Roses." But Spencer, and then Nolan, left the band (replaced by Ken Curtis and Tommy Doss, respectively), and the lineup, never all that stable, began to shift with even greater frequency. The two consistent threads were Lloyd Perryman, who grew into the roles of arranger and announcer as well and spent forty-one years with the band, and Dale Warren, who replaced Ken Curtis in 1953 and leads the current band today, an astonishing fifty-five years as a Son of the Pioneers, thirty of them as leader after Perryman's death.

The names of other men who toured and recorded as pioneers are legion: Rusty Richards, Luther Nallie, Billy Liebert, Billy Armstrong, Deuce Spriggins, Roy Lanham, Rome Johnson, Sunny Spencer, Gary LeMaster, and many, many others. In his early eighties Dale Warren still leads a fine band with a powerful trio and superb instrumentalists, carrying on the honored tradition more than seventy years after those three talented youngsters pooled their resources and created the sound of western music. The original Sons of the Pioneers were inducted into the Country Music Hall of Fame in 1980.

Hank Thompson

(1925–2007)

With his big baritone voice, innovative mixture of western swing and honky-tonk, clever songwriting, and showy stage outfits, Hank Thompson was for years one of the most vivid and successful of country music's classic stars, having racked up, in his quiet dignified way, twenty-eight top-ten hits between 1948 and 1974.

Henry William Thompson was born in Waco, Texas, and, enthralled by the cowboy songs and western movies of Gene Autry, embarked on a radio career over WACO while still in high school. Upon graduation he enlisted in the navy, which not only allowed him to continue a singing career in a limited way but also sent him to Southern Methodist University, the University of Texas, and even Princeton University to study electrical engineering.

Though he considered an engineering career upon leaving the navy, he went back to radio and, with the help of Tex Ritter, landed a contract with Capitol Records in 1947; he rewarded their faith in him when his first record, "Humpty Dumpty Heart," shot to number two, followed by hits like "Green Light" in 1948, "Whoa Sailor" in 1949, and the huge hit "The Wild Side of Life" in 1952. He was consistently on the charts throughout the 1950s with such hits as "Rub-A-Dub-Dub," "Wake Up Irene," "The New Green Light," and "The Blackboard of My Heart," and weathered the rock-and-roll years with "Squaws Along the Yukon" in 1958 and "Oklahoma Hills" in 1961.

Thompson maintained a big, impeccably dressed western swing band for years, and they were among the first country groups to appear in Las Vegas showrooms; but his distinctive swing sound and drawling baritone vocals made hit records harder to come by in the countrypolitan years. A switch to Dot Records in 1968 brought a couple of honky-tonk hits immediately: "On Tap, in the Can, or in the Bottle" and "Smoky the Bar" in 1968, but "The Older the Violin, the Sweeter the Music" in 1974 proved to be the last top-ten hit of his career.

His time high on the charts may have been over at that point, but Hank Thompson continued recording and touring, though the big band went by the wayside, replaced by the much smaller Brazos Valley Boys in later years. While slicker country music ruled in the United States, Thompson found a very appreciative audience abroad, and toured frequently overseas. In fact, he scarcely stopped touring right up until his death just weeks after his eighty-second birthday. He was inducted into the Country Music Hall of Fame in 1989.

Merle Travis

(1917–1983)

Perhaps the most prodigiously gifted entertainer in this volume, Merle Travis was one of country music's most influential and enduring musicians, songwriters, and recording artists. As if that wasn't enough, he was an innovative instrument designer, a fine vocalist, an actor, an author, and even a cartoonist.

Born in western Kentucky, Merle Robert Travis absorbed the three-finger guitar style being developed there by coal miners Ike Everly and Mose Rager, mastered it, and refined it into an instantly recognizable and profoundly influential mastery of the instrument (think Chet Atkins). Pulsing, exciting, and bluesy, it was, and is, known as "Travis picking."

Travis went professional in 1937, joining Clayton McMichen's Georgia Wildcats and then WLW in Cincinnati as a member of the Drifting Pioneers in 1938 where he did his first recording work with Grandpa Jones and the Delmore Brothers for the brand-new King label. There he met Wesley Tuttle, who spent a year in Cincinnati before returning to California. Tuttle convinced Travis to join him in Hollywood, which he did in 1944. There he immediately began appearing on radio and in films, often with the popular Tuttle.

He signed with the new Capitol label in 1946 and had a flurry of top-ten records, including "Cincinnati Lou,"

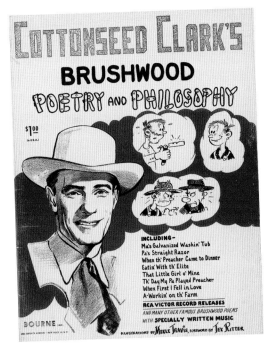

"No Vacancy," "Divorce Me C.O.D.," and other clever novelty tunes like "So Round, So Firm, So Fully Packed" and "Fat Gal." This was at the same time he was writing hit records like "Smoke, Smoke, Smoke (that Cigarette)" for Tex Williams, and playing on numerous records for West Coast acts like Tex Ritter, Eddie Dean, and others.

Having appeared in a score of B westerns and telescriptions (the forerunner of today's music videos), he was no stranger to the camera and was cast as the guitar-picking soldier in the classic film *From Here to Eternity* in 1953. As the 1950s rolled on, he appeared with Gene Autry on tour and on the *Melody Ranch* radio program, designed one of the earliest solid-body guitars, and continued to record for Capitol. Among those recordings was an album called *Folk Songs from the Hills* (many newly composed by Travis in the folk style), from which Tennessee Ernie Ford drew "Sixteen Tons," in 1955, which was to become one of the top records of the decade.

Travis worked steadily in the coming decades, but his glory days were behind him. Still, his influence as a guitarist remained steady and high, and he began to write articulate and witty articles for country music publications as well. However, Travis was a veteran of the hard-living West Coast country music scene and had abused his body severely through the years. He died of a massive coronary, much too young, in his adopted home in Oklahoma in 1983.

Merle Travis was inducted into the Country Music Hall of Fame in 1977.

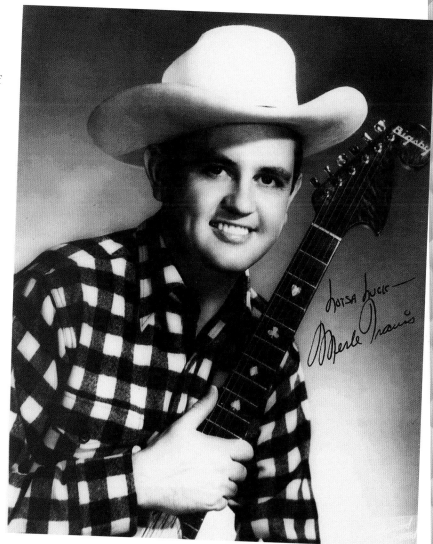

ERNEST TUBB

FOLIO OF
RECORDED
HITS No. 1

PRICE
60 CENTS

ERNEST TUBB MUSIC, INC.
7164 MELROSE AVENUE
HOLLYWOOD, CALIFORNIA

Ernest Tubb

(1914–1984)

Known and beloved as the Texas Troubadour, Ernest Dale Tubb of Crisp, Texas, began his career under the spell of Jimmie Rodgers; in fact, he was so devoted to the Singing Brakeman that he befriended Rodgers' widow, who in turn sponsored the young man's career and gave him one of Rodgers' rare guitars, and even got him a record deal with Victor, Rodgers' label.

However, it was not until he developed his own distinctive sound and style that Ernest Tubb signed with Decca Records, where he began a series of hits with "Blue Eyed Elaine" in 1940 followed by his all-time best seller, "Walking the Floor Over You" the following year. This led to musical roles in a couple of Charles Starrett westerns and then to membership at the Grand Ole Opry in 1943, where he remained as one of its major stars for the next thirty-one years.

He and his band, the Texas Troubadours, racked up an impressive string of hits in the middle to late 1940s, including "Soldier's Last Letter" in 1944, "Careless Darlin'" in 1945, "Rainbow at Midnight," "Filipino Baby," and "Driving Nails in My Coffin" in 1946, "Have You Ever Been Lonely" in 1948, "Slipping Around" and "Blue Christmas" in 1949, and "You Don't Have to Be a

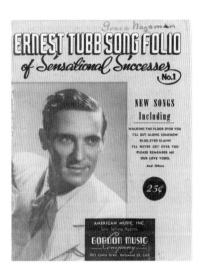

Baby to Cry" and "Remember Me (I'm the One Who Loves You)" in 1950. All featured his deep Texas drawl and the endearing approximation of pitch, trailing off at the end of phrases, which was frequently imitated but was enormously appealing to generations of record buyers at the same time.

Tubb began a series of good-natured duet records with Red Foley in 1949, producing half a dozen hits until 1953, including "Tennessee Border #2," "Don't Be Ashamed of Your Age," and "Goodnight Irene." He was fond of the duet form and also recorded with the Andrews Sisters, the Wilburn Brothers, and Loretta Lynn in his long career. He opened the Ernest Tubb Record Shop in 1947 and began a live radio broadcast every Saturday night following the *Grand Ole Opry* called *Midnite Jamboree*, a show that continues to this day; after the *Grand Ole Opry* itself, it is the second-longest continually running radio show in history.

Tall, courtly, and gracious, Tubb grew into the role of elder statesman and national symbol for the Texas side of country music as the years passed and was a steady presence on country radio well into the 1970s, with his last major hit being "Thanks a Lot" in 1963. He also hosted his own syndicated television show from 1965 to 1968 and was indefatigable when it came to road work: he toured almost nonstop until emphysema finally slowed him down in the 1980s.

Generous as a mentor, he made minor celebrities out of band members like Billy Byrd, Leon Rhodes, and Buddy Emmons; and two Texas Troubadours, with Tubb's help and encouragement, went on to long careers as hit-making soloists: Cal Smith and Jack Greene.

Long a national symbol and ambassador for country music, Tubb was elected to the Country Music Hall of Fame in 1965.

Jimmy Wakely

(1914–1982)

Though he may be best remembered as one of the great singing cowboys of film, Jimmy Wakely's career crossed many boundaries, touched on many styles, and attained success in many arenas.

At the start he was a pure western singer. Born in Mineola, Arkansas, and raised in Oklahoma, he grew up with the records of Jimmie Rodgers but fell in love with the sound of the Sons of the Pioneers. He, Scotty Harrell, and Johnny Bond formed a harmony group (in later years called the Jimmy Wakely Trio or the Rough Riders) and played over WKY in Oklahoma City, where in 1940 the trio auditioned for Gene Autry while on a tour and were encouraged to try their luck in Hollywood.

Though success did not come overnight, it came, with small film parts, recording contracts for each member of the trio (Decca for Wakely and Columbia for Bond and Dick Rinehart, who had replaced Harrell), and eventually radio work as Gene Autry's harmony singers on his CBS *Melody Ranch* radio show. Bond landed a recording contract first, and his "Cimarron" became a western classic, but Wakely too was a fine songwriter. His "Too Late" (1941) was the first country hit record for members of the trio, and with its success Wakely left the trio to try a solo career.

Though not a big, rugged man, Wakely's good looks and beautiful voice got him singing parts in numerous B westerns before being signed by Monogram in 1944 to star in a singing

SONGS
Jimmy Wakely
SINGS

THIRTY-FIVE CENTS

COMPLETE
WORDS
MUSIC

Arranged
PIANO   VOICE

JIMMY WAKELY

SONGS OF THE RANGE

Also Colorful Illustrations
and Action Photographs

TO A PAL
FROM
Jimmy Wakely

FAIRWAY MUSIC CO.
1651 Cosmo Street
Hollywood 28, California

cowboy series, which, by the time it was over in 1950, amounted to some twenty-eight films.

Having had some success on Decca, he moved over to Capitol Records in 1948 and had a number-one record (number ten pop) with Eddie Dean's "One Has My Name, the Other Has My Heart," which featured uncredited harmony vocals by Colleen Summers (soon to be known as Mary Ford of Les Paul and Mary Ford). He scored a second number one that year with Floyd Tillman's "I Love You So Much It Hurts," and had yet another top-ten hit in the duet style (this time with Velma Williams, again uncredited) with "Till the End of the World" in 1949. This led producer Lee Gillette to dream up the notion of pairing the cowboy singer with an established pop star, in this case Margaret Whiting, whose sassy voice contrasted and comple-mented Wakely's smooth Crosbyesque baritone.

Their first effort, Tillman's "Slipping Around," shot to number one in both country and pop, the cheerful approach to a formerly taboo subject taking the nation by storm—so much so that the flip side of the single, Hank Williams' "Wedding Bells," reached number six country and number thirty pop at the same time! The unlikely pair—both of whom were hugely gifted vocal-ists and harmonized beautifully with each other—recorded frequently for the next few years. While they never found that million-selling magic again, they had a nice string of hits, including an inevitable "I'll Never Slip Around Again," "Broken Down Merry Go Round," "The God's Were Angry With Me," and "I Don't Want to Be Free." In addition, Wakely had several hits of his own, including "Mona Lisa" long before Nat Cole, "My Heart Cries for You," and "Beautiful Brown Eyes."

Oddly, his chart records fell off a cliff after 1951; he was never seen in those lofty regions again, although he recorded for Capitol, then Coral, and then Decca as the fifties rolled by. Still, he could hardly have been busier: he toured (often with Bob Hope), produced records, began a CBS radio show, found a few more secondary acting roles, appeared on television (he was one of the stars of ABC-TVs *Five Star Jamboree* in 1961), and pioneered country music being featured in Nevada showrooms.

In later years he became something of an elder statesman for western music and even created his own record label to keep his music and the music of some of his best friends (Bond, Eddie Dean, Merle Travis, and others) alive when it looked in danger of being forgotten. Emphysema brought his life to a close in 1982; he did not live to see the resurgence in western music and cowboy culture he had fought so hard to preserve.

Kitty Wells

(1919 –)

Reserved, gracious Kitty Wells, the Queen of Country Music, was an unlikely star: a soulful singer with a piercing, tearful alto in an era of lush female vocalists (think Patti Page), a woman in an age dominated by male singers, a young mother and wife already well into her thirties with several recordings behind her that received little notice, she burst seemingly out of nowhere to take the country by storm when "It Wasn't God Who Made Honky-Tonk Angels" rocketed to number one in July 1952.

But Muriel Deason Wright had been working for fifteen years at becoming an overnight success, appearing with her sisters and a cousin as the Deason Sisters over local radio in her hometown of Nashville, Tennessee, in the late 1930s. A teenage bride, she married Johnnie Wright in 1937, and appeared with him and his sister as Johnnie Wright

and the Harmony Girls before he teamed up with Jack Anglin to form Johnnie and Jack, an outstanding duet team that reunited after World War II and joined the *Louisiana Hayride,* later coming to the Grand Ole Opry with the success of their hit record "Poison Love" in 1952.

Muriel, who adopted the name of an old folk song for her stage name, was part of the Johnnie and Jack stage show (while raising three children as well) and, like them, recorded for RCA, but, unlike them, without success. Her first recording for Decca, "It Wasn't God Who Made Honky-Tonk Angels," an answer to Hank Thompson's "The Wild Side of Life," became a sensation and launched her acclaimed career.

Hit records abounded in the early to mid-1950s, including "Paying for that Back Street Affair" and "Hey Joe" in 1953, "Release Me" in 1954, "Makin' Believe," "Lonely Side of Town," "There's Poison in Your Heart," and "Whose Shoulder Will You Cry On?" in 1955, "Searching" in 1956, and "I Can't Stop Loving You" in 1958. In addition, she scored several top-ten hits in

LEFT: Kitty Wells with Johnnie Wright, left, and Jack Anglin.

duets with Red Foley, including "As Long As I Live" in 1955, "You and Me" in 1956, and their number one record, "One By One," in 1954.

Despite her plaintive country sound she remained country music's queen through the rock-and-roll years, with songs like "Amigo's Guitar" (1959), and her last number one record, "Heartbreak USA" (1961), making her a consistent chart presence throughout the 1960s and well into the 1970s.

With the death of Jack Anglin in 1963, Kitty and Johnnie (who, by this time, had taken to the spelling "Johnny") formed the Kitty Wells–Johnny Wright Traveling Show with their talented children. (All had successful recording careers, and Bobby had a career as an actor as well.) They continued touring quite actively well into the 1990s. She was elected into the Country Music Hall of Fame in 1976 and was presented with a Lifetime Achievement Award at the Grammy Awards in 1991.

Hank Williams

(1923–1953)

Country music's iconic tragic figure quickly became a legend bigger than life following his startling early death at twenty-nine; for three decades or more, his meteoric rise and fall, and the transparent intensity of his music, seemed to define country music as it broke from its regional confines to become a national phenomenon.

Hiram Williams was born deep in rural central Alabama, near the Georgia state line. Barely into his teens, the skinny young man, heavily influenced by the sound of Roy Acuff, was forming bands and playing with older, hard-living musicians. After World War II he had developed a big regional following around Montgomery and made connections with legendary songwriter and publisher Fred Rose in Nashville, who helped to nurture the career and music of the charismatic but already unreliable young man. Rose signed him to a songwriting contract, worked with him on his songs and on his life, and got him a record contract with Sterling Records in 1946 and a spot on the *Louisiana Hayride* in 1948.

Williams had a number of charted records for the new MGM label in 1948 and 1949, including "Move It on Over" and "Honky-Tonkin'," but it was the huge success of his lonesome yodeling "Lovesick Blues," an old vaudeville tune, that sparked an invitation to the Grand Ole Opry in 1949 and further hit records like "Mansion on the Hill," "Wedding Bells," "Mind Your Own Business," and "Lost Highway." Nineteen-fifty and 1951 proved to be the apex of his career as every record he released charted high, and many of the songs, nearly all of which he wrote, became standards, including "Long Gone Lonesome Blues," "Cold, Cold Heart," "I Can't Help It," "Hey, Good Looking" and "Why Don't You Love Me?"

Win Again"), Williams was released by the Opry; he disbanded his Drifting Cowboys band, worked little, and was in and out of rehab. His marriage in shambles, he moved in with the up-and-coming Ray Price in one of several efforts to stop the free fall. Remarriage and a back operation—which proved unsuccessful—seemed to stave off the inevitable for a time, but it was too little too late for the tortured young man.

Ironically, his record of "I'll Never Get Out of This World Alive" was the number one record in the country the night he passed away, in the back of a chauffeured Cadillac, on the way to a personal appearance in Ohio on New Year's Day of 1953. His frail body simply gave out after a short but intense life of alcohol and prescription drug abuse.

Posthumous record releases proved to be his biggest hits yet and secured his status as one of country music's icons. "Your Cheatin' Heart," "Kaw-Liga," and "Take These Chains from My Heart" dominated the charts in 1953 and added to the oeuvre and the legend.

Long considered unreliable, his personal life spun out of control the following year. While huge chart records continued unabated ("Half as Much," "Jambalaya," "Settin' the Woods on Fire," and "You For a time his vivid story of meteoric rise an fall, and the intensely personal nature of his songwriting, engraved the image of Hank Williams as the face of country music in American popular culture. In recent years, more balanced looks by dispassionate historians have toned down the hagiography of his talent and the fascination with the lurid aspects of his very public life, so often recapitulated in his songs, and have produced more balanced studies of the man and his music, which remains piercing, raw, and vivid a half century after his death. He was inducted into the Country Music Hall of Fame in 1961.

BELOW: Don Helms, left, Sammy Pruett, Hank Williams, Jerry Rivers, and Hilous Butrum.

Bob Wills

(1905–1975)

The charismatic champion of western swing was born James Robert Wills near Kosse, Texas, to a family of musicians; it is little surprise that he and three of his brothers would all have long professional careers. Taking the pioneer fiddle music of his childhood and blending it with small band jazz and, later, big band swing, he forged a danceable, exciting, musically adventurous style that came to be called western swing. To this day, his large body of songs remains the symbol of the style.

Historians of the style are quick to point out that he did not create it alone; no one in a band setting can do so. But he and the pool of talented musicians with whom he surrounded himself certainly were the prime movers in this unique and still-vital genre of country music, and he and the Texas Playboys remain its enduring symbol.

Wills began recording as early as 1929 but first found success as a founding member of the Light Crust Doughboys (sponsored by Burrus Mills, maker of Light Crust Flour), which featured not only his somewhat rough hewn but exciting fiddle playing but the smooth vocals of Milton Brown. Brown left the group in 1932 and went on to rising success with his own pioneering western swing band, the Musical Brownies, before being killed in an automobile accident.

Wills replaced Brown with another superb vocalist, Tommy Duncan, and the two left the Doughboys in 1934, winding up in Tulsa where for the next half dozen years they became one of the most popular bands in America. They began recording for ARC in 1935 and were unafraid to tackle anything, from folk songs and fiddle tunes to the latest pop hits, all done in easygoing,

TEX RITTER TAKE ME BACK TO OKLAHOMA

featuring
BOB WILLS
A Monogram
PICTURE

U.S. MAIL

danceable swing. As big bands became the rage in that era, Wills expanded his Texas Playboys to as many as eighteen pieces, with a full horn section. Yet they never got too slick sounding, for Duncan's sun-warmed voice embodied the feel of the Southwest, and Wills' effervescent asides during the songs became a trademark. There was always the edgy feeling of incipient chaos. It was during these years that most of the classic songs of the style were recorded, including "Right or Wrong," "A Maiden's Prayer," "Spanish Two-Step," "Old Fashioned Love," "Ida Red," "Steel Guitar Rag," "Time Changes Everything," "Dusty Skies," "Miss Molly," and, of course, "San Antonio Rose," which swept the country during the war years.

The draft decimated the band, and they broke up for a short time, but after Wills' release, the Texas Playboys re-formed on the West Coast, where demand for dances was enormous. Having been to Hollywood several times to appear as musicians in western films with Penny Singleton, Tex Ritter, and Russell Hayden, Wills and the boys were eager to relocate. This proved to be the most financially successful time in his career, as hits kept coming, including vocal remakes on "New San Antonio Rose" and "New Spanish Two Step" (originally recorded as fiddle tunes), and newly minted classics-to-be like "Smoke on the Water," "Hang Your Head in Shame," "Silver Dew on the Blue Grass Tonight," "Roly-Poly," and "Sugar Moon."

Not long after the war, interest in western swing was in decline. Wills had several more hit records after moving to MGM records in 1947, including "Bubbles in My Beer," "Keeper of My Heart," and the classic "Faded Love"; but Tommy Duncan left the band to start his own group, and continued sagging attendance caused Wills to relocate to Oklahoma in 1949. He had already dropped the horns for a smaller, string-oriented band (two or three fiddles, electric guitar, and electric steel guitar and rhythm section). Though he stayed busy, the late 1950s and 1960s found him sounding increasingly dated and plagued by ill health. He finally disbanded what was left of the band by 1967.

He was not forgotten by the music community, however. Merle Haggard's tribute album introduced him and his music to a whole new generation, and he was elected to the Country Music Hall of Fame in 1968. A stroke later that year ended his performing career, though he held on, in increasingly poor health and finally in a fifteen-month coma, until the end in 1975.

FACING: Tex Ritter, left, Bob Wills, Leon McAuliffe, Eldon Shamblin, Johnny Lee Wills, Son Lansford, and Wayne Johnson.

Faron Young

(1932–1996)

A larger-than-life character's character, Faron Young was at one time one of country music's brightest lights. He moved the raw honky-tonk sound of Hank Williams into the rockabilly era, and then straight into the smooth and glossy Nashville Sound era that followed.

Born in Shreveport, Louisiana, Young met Webb Pierce, star of the *Louisiana Hayride*, in Shreveport while Young was still a teen. He began touring with Pierce and was appearing on the *Hayride* himself by 1951. After a couple of sides on the Gotham label, he signed with Capitol Records and moved to Nashville in 1952 on the heels of the release of "Goin' Steady," which hit number two in the country charts in 1953.

Young was drafted shortly thereafter, but his career was not to be denied. He continued to perform and record while in the army, and upon his release in November 1954, "If You Ain't Lovin'" was climbing the charts, eventually to peak, like "Goin' Steady," at number two. His early sound was heavily influenced by Hank Williams, but he incrementally developed his own sound and style, and a dazzling array of hits followed: "Live Fast, Love Hard, Die Young" and "All Right" in 1955, "I've Got Five Dollars and It's Saturday Night," and the first recording of "Sweet Dreams" in 1956, "Alone With You" and "That's the Way I Feel" in 1958.

Rock and roll damaged Young's career, as was the case with many country artists: he claimed he went

It's Four In The Morning

Words and Music by JERRY CHESNUT

Recorded by
FARON YOUNG
on Mercury

20p

BURLINGTON MUSIC CO. LTD.
sole selling agents:
MUSIC SALES LTD.,
78 Newman Street, London, W.1.

from a $225,000 income to $75,000 in the space of a year, but that was still a very good living in the 1950s. He continued to record for Capitol and appeared in a handful of low-grade westerns and drive-in musicals as well.

When the Nashville Sound came in as an antidote to rock, Young jumped in with both feet, becoming a suave balladeer, trading in his rhinestones for tailored suits. He began a new assault on the charts with "Hello Walls" in 1961, which went to number one (and number twelve on the pop charts), and then, switching to Mercury Records, scored another half dozen top ten-hits with that label through 1971, including classics like "Yellow Bandana," "Wine Me Up," "Unmitigated Gall," "Step Aside," "Leaving and Saying Goodbye," and his last number one record, "It's Four in the Morning," in 1971.

Young became a businessman, real estate entrepreneur, and publisher (Music City News) as his active performing career wound down, and he made his final recordings, for MCA and then for the independent Step One, in the 1980s. Yet instead of energizing him, these new challenges only seemed to deepen his depression over the fading of his career. That and his failing health caused him to lose heart entirely in the 1990s. Though outwardly still vigorous, colorful, and irascible at sixty-four,

FARON YOUNG

"THE YOUNG SHERIFF" AND HIS

STAR OF . . .

★ WSM's GRAND OLE OPRY
★ RADIO
★ TELEVISION
★ MOVIES
★ PERSONAL APPEARANCE

COUNTRY DEPUTIES

Young's private torments caused him to take his own life just a couple of weeks before Christmas in 1996. He was inducted into the Country Music Hall of Fame in 2000.

Bibliography

The Stars

Autry, Gene, and Mickey Herskowitz. *Back in the Saddle Again.* Doubleday, 1976.

Bond, Johnny. *The Tex Ritter Story.* Chappell, 1976.

———. *Thirty Years on the Road with Gene Autry: Reflections.* Riverwood Press, 2007.

Cooper, Daniel. *Lefty Frizzell: The Honky-Tonk Life of Country Music's Greatest Singer.* Little, Brown, 1995.

Cusic, Don. *Gene Autry.* McFarland & Company 2007.

———. *Eddy Arnold: I'll Hold You in My Heart.* Thomas Nelson, 1997.

Delmore, Alton. *Truth Is Stranger than Publicity.* Country Music Foundation Press, 1977.

Diekman, Diane. *Live Fast, Love Hard: The Faron Young Story.* University of Illinois Press, 2007.

Escott, Colin. *Hank Williams.* Back Bay Books, 2004.

George-Warren, Holly. *Public Cowboy #1: The Life and Times of Gene Autry.* Oxford University Press, 2007.

Griffis, Ken. *Hear My Song: The Story of the Celebrated Sons of the Pioneers.* Norken, 1998.

Hall, Wade. *Hell Bent for Music: The Life of Pee Wee King.* University Press of Kentucky, 1996.

Hemphill, Paul. *Lovesick Blues: The Life of Hank Williams.* Penguin, 2005.

Jones, Louis B., and Charles K. Wolfe. *Everybody's Grandpa: Fifty Years Behind the Mike.* University of Tennessee Press, 1984.

Jones, Loyal. *Radio's Kentucky Mountain Boy: Bradley Kincaid.* Berea College Appalachian Center, 1980.

Montana, Patsy, and Jane Frost. *Patsy Montana: Cowboy's Sweetheart.* McFarland & Company, 2002.

O'Neill, Bill. *Tex Ritter: America's Most Beloved Cowboy.* Eakin, 1997.

O'Neill, Bill and Fred Goodwin. *The Sons of the Pioneers.* Eakin, 2001.

Palmer, Jack. *Vernon Dalhart: First Star of Country Music.* Mainspring Press, 2005.

Paris, Mike, and Chris Comber. *Jimmie the Kid: The Life of Jimmie Rodgers.* Eddison Musicbooks, 1977.

Porterfield, Nolan. *Jimmie Rodgers.* University of Illinois Press, 1977.

Pruett, Barbara J. *Marty Robbins: Race Cars and Country Music.* Rowman & Littlefield, 2007.

Pugh, Ronnie. *Ernest Tubb: The Texas Troubadour.* Duke University Press, 1997.

Russell, Tony. *Country Music Originals: The Legends and the Lost.* Oxford University Press, 2007.

Schlappi, Elizabeth. *Roy Acuff: The Smokey Mountain Boy.* Pelican Publishing, 1993.

Smith, Richard. *Can't You Hear Me Callin': The Life of Bill Monroe, Father of Bluegrass.* Little, Brown, 2000.

Snow, Hank. *The Hank Snow Story.* University of Illinois Press, 1997.

Streissguth, Michael. *Eddy Arnold: Pioneer of the Nashville Sound.* Schirmer, 1997.

———. *From a Moth to a Flame: The Jim Reeves Story.* Thomas Nelson, 1998.

Townsend, Charles A. *San Antonio Rose: The Life and Music of Bob Wills.* University of Illinois Press, 1977.

Wakely, Linda Lee. *See Ya Up There Baby: The Jimmy Wakely Story.* Shasta, 1992.

Weill, Gus. *You Are My Sunshine: The Jimmie Davis Story.* Word, 1977.

Williams, Roger. *Sing a Sad Song: The Story of Hank Williams.* University of Illinois Press, 1981.

Wolfe, Charles K. *Classic Country: Legends of Country Music.* Taylor & Francis, 2001.

———. *In Close Harmony: The Story of the Louvin Brothers.* University Press of Mississippi, 1996.

Zwonitzer, Mark, and Charles Hirshberg. *Will You Miss Me When I'm Gone?: The Carter Family and Their Legacy in American Music.* Simon and Schuster, 2002.

The Story

Bufwack, Mary, and Robert K. Oermann, *Finding Her Voice: The Saga of Women in Country Music*. Crown, 1993.

Escott, Colin. *The Grand Ole Opry: The Making of an American Icon*. Center Street, 2006.

———. *Lost Highway*. Smithsonian Institution Press, 2003.

Green, Douglas B. *Country Roots: The Origins of Country Music*. Hawthorne, 1976.

Kingsbury, Paul. *Country: The Sound and the Musicians*. Abbeville Press, 1988.

———. *The Encyclopedia of Country Music: The Ultimate Guide to the Music*. Oxford University Press, 2004.

Kingsbury, Paul, and Alanna Nash, eds. *Will the Circle Be Unbroken: Country Music in America*. DK Publishing, 2006.

Laird, Tracey E. W. *Louisiana Hayride: Radio and Roots along the Red River*. Oxford University Press, 2004.

Malone, Bill C. *Country Music, U.S.A*. University of Texas Press, 2002.

———. *Don't Get Above Your Raisin': Country Music and the Southern Working Class*. University of Illinois Press, 2002.

———. *Singing Cowboys and Musical Mountaineers: Southern Culture and the Roots of Country Music*. University of Georgia Press, 1993.

Pecknold, Diane. *Selling the Sound: The Rise of the Country Music Industry*. Duke University Press, 2007.

Peterson, Richard A. *Creating Country Music: Fabricating Authenticity*. University of Chicago Press, 1997.

Time-Life Books, eds. *Classic Country: The Golden Age of Country Music, the 20s through the 70s*. Time-Life, 2001.

———, eds. *Legends of Classic Country*. Time-Life, 2000.

Tosches, Nick. *Country: The Twisted Roots of Rock 'n' Roll*. Da Capo Press, 1996.

Wolfe, Charles K. *A Good Natured Riot: The Birth of the Grand Ole Opry*. Vanderbilt University Press/Country Music Foundation Press, 1999.

The Stats

Russell, Tony, and Bob Pinson. *Country Music Records: A Discography 1921–1942*. Oxford University Press, 2003.

Whitburn, Joel. *Top Country Songs 1944–2005*. Record Research, 2006.

The Styles

Boyd, Jean A. *The Jazz of the Southwest*. University of Texas Press, 1998.

Cantwell, Robert. *Bluegrass Breakdown: The Making of the Old Southern Sound*. University of Illinois Press, 2002.

Ginell, Cary. *Milton Brown and the Founding of Western Swing*. University of Illinois Press, 1994.

Goldsmith, Thomas. *The Bluegrass Reader*. University of Illinois Press, 2004.

Green, Douglas B. *Singing Cowboys*. Gibbs Smith, Publisher, 2006.

———. *Singing in the Saddle: The History of the Singing Cowboy*. Vanderbilt University Press/Country Music Foundation Press, 2002.

Kienzle, Rich. *Southwest Shuffle: Pioneers of Honky-Tonk, Western Swing, and Country Jazz*. Taylor and Francis, 2003.

Rosenberg, Neil V. *Bluegrass: A History*. University of Illinois Press, 2005.

Stanfield, Peter R. *Horse Opera: The Strange History of the 1930s Singing Cowboys*. University of Illinois Press, 2002.

Trevino, Geronimo. *Dance Halls and Last Calls: The History of Texas Country Music*. Rowman & Littlefield, 2002.

Thanks!

With deepest gratitude to Michelle Witte and Madge Baird and Gibbs Smith for their guidance and enthusiasm, and to Lee Rowe at the Country Music Foundation Library and Media Center.